VEGETABLE MAGIC
with
MICROWAVE COOKING

SO-EKZ-609

by Phe Laws

Hidden House Publications
Palo Alto, Ca.

This book is dedicated first to my husband, my son, and my daughter who have spent many years enthusiastically eating my cooking and supporting my writing endeavors. Very special mention also goes to Wayne Rowley who has encouraged and helped me in my effort to become the best possible microwave cooking teacher and who has been my friend.

Thank you, all.

Acknowledgements

Luciano	Book Design
Sharon Kaplan-Weiner	Editor
Chuck C. Koehler	Photography
Publications Services	Composition

Distribution

To Book Stores	To All Others
Quick Fox, Inc.	Craft Trends, Inc.
33 West 60th St.	505 Hamilton Ave., Suite 105
N.Y., N.Y. 10023	Palo Alto, Ca. 94301
(212) 246-0325	(415) 327-5501

TABLE OF CONTENTS

NOTE TO THE COOK

This cookbook is the result of teaching "Vegetable Cookery" classes at Ohlone College. It was one of the most satisfying classes possible and was great fun to teach. When a 50-year-old woman came to me at the end of the class and enthusiastically stated that "For the first time in my life I am eating vegetables and enjoying them!"; when a young man said in amazement "I never knew you could eat vegetables and be so satisfied."; when many similar statements were made; it was brought home to me how very much a cookbook on vegetable cookery was needed. Since the microwave oven is the best possible way to cook vegetables and since microwave cooking is my specialty, the two were blended into this book.

A wide range of vegetables has been included, as wide a range as possible without resorting to specialty shops that are located only in limited areas. Thus vegetables such as Jerusalem artichokes and celeriac were included while vegetables such as bitter melon and daikon were omitted. You could, using this book, actually serve a different vegetable every day for a month without once repeating. Using the recipes and the EXTRA SERVING SUGGESTIONS, which are really one-line recipes, you could use a different recipe every day for seven months. Using the SAUCES AND SUCH suggestions, which are also recipes, you could go on without repeating for well over a year. The next time you are tempted to serve peas or corn with a dab of butter added, don't. Pick up this book and let a little imagination take over. You will be delighted that you did for vegetables will take on new life.

For the VEGETARIAN'S INFORMATION the recipes for some sauces include chicken bouillon concentrate. While it would cause some flavor change, the bouillon concentrate may be omitted, if you desire. Since vegetarians differ greatly in their strictness, there has been no effort to designate which dishes are strictly vegetarian. Some people who call themselves vegetarian will eat no milk products or eggs, as well as no meat or meat extracts. Others will eat milk products and eggs but no meat or meat extracts. Some will even go so far as to eat fish and poultry, but no meat and still say they are vegetarian. Reading of ingredients will be necessary to see if the recipe fulfills your requirements.

With each recipe I have included an estimate of the PREPARATION TIME. This time includes the time needed to prepare the food as well as cook it. Thus when there is plenty of time, you may choose a food that takes a while to prepare. When you are in a hurry, look for those recipes with short preparation times noted. Quite a few recipes need less than 20 minutes to prepare. A very few foods need chilling before serving. Chilling time is not included in the preparation time figure.

No instructions on TURNING or ROTATING have been given. In some ovens, no turning is necessary; in others, frequent turning or rotating is needed. Follow the instructions for your unit.

With each recipe I have also included a space for you to record your ACTUAL COOKING TIME experienced when cooking that dish in your oven. Ovens differ greatly in their cooking speed. Wattage is of prime importance. A Whirlpool Model No. 7400 and a Litton Model No. 420 were used in testing the recipes in this book. Both units are rated at 650 watts yet one unit took 5 seconds longer per minute of cooking time to do the same job as the other one did. Cooking time in these recipes is geared to an oven that will bring one standard measuring cup of tap water (56° F. or 13° C.) to a boil in 2 minutes and 50 seconds. If your oven is rated at 700 watts, it will probably be necessary to subtract about 4 to 5 seconds per minute of cooking time. If your oven has 600 watts of cooking power, add 4 to 5 seconds per minute of cooking time. A 550 watt oven will need 8 to 10 seconds per minute of cooking time added. A 450 watt oven (most of the smaller, less expensive ovens are rated at 450 watts) needs 15 to 20 seconds per minute of cooking time added. Only experience with your oven will allow you to know how much time, per minute of cooking time, to add or to subtract from the norm.

6

I have also provided a summary MICROWAVE COOKING GUIDE. You will find it useful and informative. It is intended as a supplement to the cooking instructions provided by the manufacturer of your particular microwave oven. Please read it through. It will tell you many important things about microwave cooking.

One last word on the cooking times and directions given in this book. As you read through the recipes, it will be apparent that I appreciate texture as well as taste in vegetables. The timing is geared to preserving texture; the microwave oven is geared to preserving flavor. Nutrition is also important which is why liquid is not drained from vegetables and discarded. Remember, it is much better to get your vitamins and minerals from vegetables than it is from a pill.

Bon Appétit,

PHE'S GUIDE
TO GREAT MICROWAVE COOKING

INTRODUCTION

When a person brings a microwave oven home, the first thing he or she wants to know is "How do I use it?" or "How can I cook in it?" or just plain "What do I do now?"

First of all, I hope you have read and will continue to review the information and instructions contained in the manufacturer's microwave cookbook usually provided with your oven. Microwave cooking techniques are sometimes different from those in conventional cooking. Often, though, they are quite similar, with slight, but very important, differences.

In the guide which follows, I have attempted to share with you the more important things to know about the microwave cooking process and the cooking methods that have worked best for me. On the next page you will find a table of contents of the topics I have covered in this abbreviated guide.

When following my recipe instructions, keep in mind that:

- all cooking is to be done in your microwave oven unless otherwise stated
- cooking times given are always the least possible time in which foods can cook
- you must allow for residual cooking
- if turning of foods is needed in your oven, turn as necessary
- you should always apply basic microwave cooking techniques.

CONTENTS

8

HEAT PRODUCTION

First, it helps to know a little about microwave ovens and how they work so you can understand what is happening and why. Microwaves are actually radio-frequency waves and the manufacturers of them are licensed to operate on certain specific radio frequencies by the Federal Communications Commission. These radio-frequency waves are called microwaves because they are very short in length.

When microwaves enter anything containing water molecules, the water molecules are activated and move about so rapidly that they hit and rub against other molecules in the food, producing heat by friction on the molecular level. If you were to rub your hands together, back and forth rapidly ten times, you would generate a lot of heat quickly. It is this effect that produces great heat so quickly in food in the microwave oven.

RESIDUAL COOKING

All foods, no matter how they are cooked, have residual cooking. This is the cooking that takes place in the food after it is removed from the heat source—the cooking that is caused by the heat in the food itself. The heavier and denser a piece of food is, the more residual cooking takes place. In microwave cooking there is a greater amount of residual cooking than in conventional cooking.

During microwave cooking the water molecules gain momentum and it takes time for that momentum to be used, even after the microwave oven has shut off. While the momentum is being used, more heat continues to be produced. When a roast is taken from the microwave oven, its internal temperature can climb as much as 15 degrees in the following 15 to 20 minutes. Remember this in microwave cooking. Slightly undercook foods so that they won't be overcooked by the time they are eaten.

HEAT PENETRATION

Microwaves do not cook foods from the inside out. If they did, a rare roast could not be prepared in the microwave oven. As microwaves penetrate the surfaces of foods, many are "absorbed" by the first water molecules and changed into heat. Many of the microwaves that go beyond the surface are "absorbed" by water molecules just below the surface. The further a water molecule is from the surface, the less chance it has of "absorbing" a microwave and converting it into heat. Thus the greatest amount of heat is produced at the surface; the deeper one goes into the food, the less heat has been generated.

Most of the heat is produced in the outer half inch of the food. A moderate amount is produced in the second half inch. Very little heat is produced in the third half inch. This is why it is said, "Microwaves have an effective heat-producing-penetration of one-half inch to one inch into the food." The heat that is generated by the microwaves must then reach the center of the food by conduction. Conduction of heat through food is very slow. Stirring of food, whenever possible, helps to distribute the heat evenly throughout the food and allows quicker and more even cooking.

10

STIRRING—WHY AND WHEN

In conventional cooking there are three reasons for stirring. In microwave cooking there are only two. The first reason for stirring is to redistribute the heat evenly. By stirring, the colder food in the center of the dish is mixed with the hotter food on the surface. In microwave cooking, more stirring of this type is needed than in conventional cooking because the heat is produced faster in the outer surfaces. Often you will be directed to stir something in the microwave oven that normally is not stirred at all in conventional cooking.

The second reason for stirring is to keep a thickening agent in suspension. When you make a gravy, sauce, or pudding, the liquid is usually thickened with flour, cornstarch, or some other starch material. If you do not stir, the starch settles to the bottom of the liquid and makes a heavy, gummy layer. This type of stirring is done in both conventional and microwave cooking. In microwave cooking, several stirrings during the LAST half of the cooking period are all that are needed. Actually that is all that is needed in conventional cooking to keep the starch in suspension.

All the extra stirring needed in conventional cooking when making gravies, sauces, or puddings is not to keep the starch in suspension but is to prevent sticking, scorching, or burning of the food. This is the third reason for stirring. It is the one that is not needed in microwave cooking.

COOL COOKING AND EASY DISHWASHING

Microwave cooking is called cool cooking because the heat is produced in the food and not in the oven or the cooking utensils. **11** Neither the oven nor the utensils have any heat of their own. This does not mean they won't get warm or even hot. If a cup has boiling water in it, the cup will pick up heat from the water. So it is in microwave cooking.

The oven will pick up some heat from the food cooking in it. After prolonged cooking, the walls of the oven will usually be cool enough to touch. Sometimes the tray where the food actually sets will get too hot to touch. The tray picks up more heat than the oven walls because it is in direct contact with the hottest part of the food or the food container. In comparison to the heat given off by a conventional oven, this amount of heat is minimal.

A cooking container, however, does not get hotter than the food that is cooking in it. A covered container will get hotter than an uncovered one because steam is trapped in it. Because the container does not get hotter than the food that is cooking in it, food does not stick, scorch, or burn onto the container. (Browning trays are an exception to this.)

Try this experiment. Make a cup of hot chocolate on your conventional burner. Make a cup of hot chocolate in the microwave oven. Compare your cooking containers. The one from your conventional burner needs scouring. The one from the microwave oven needs rinsing.

FOOD SHRINKAGE AND CRUSTING

There will be much less food shrinkage and crusting in the microwave oven than in a conventional oven. Shrinkage is especially noticeable in meat in conventional cooking because conventional ovens are full of very hot, very dry air. This hot, dry air evaporates large quantities of moisture from foods. This is the cause of shrinkage in roasts. Roasts cooked in the microwave oven will have very little shrinkage and will remain juicier and more moist.

It is this same *dehydration* that causes crusting of foods cooked conventionally. Foods cooked in the microwave oven have little crusting. For this reason some foods cannot be cooked in the microwave oven. This includes popovers, cream puffs, and angel food cakes. On other foods, if there is not enough crusting from the microwave oven to suit you, it is possible to offset this by putting the food under the broiler of your conventional oven for a few minutes after cooking it by microwave.

Drop cookies and pizza do not crust properly in the microwave oven for a different reason. These foods need to be cooked on a very hot surface to achieve their usual crusting and texture. There is no hot surface to cook on in the microwave oven. Pizza can be reheated in the microwave oven, though.

CAN I USE MY METAL PANS?

Three things can happen to a microwave once it enters the oven cavity. First of all it can be *transmitted*, that is, it can pass through something without affecting that thing and without being affected by that thing. Anything that can transmit microwaves is said to be transparent to microwaves. This includes the air in the oven and all the containers that are used for cooking. Metal is not transparent to microwaves.

12

Secondly, a microwave can be *reflected*. Metal reflects microwaves. This is why metal cooking utensils cannot be used. Microwave cooking is efficient when the food is exposed to the microwaves from all possible directions and angles. Metal utensils block out most of this exposure and greatly reduce the efficiency of the oven. In many ovens metal will also reflect microwaves back to the magnetron tube—the tube that generates the microwaves. This will damage or destroy the magnetron tube. This tube is quite expensive. Continuous metal, as in the metal walls of the oven, does not cause arcing. Discontinuous metal, as in the metal pans, in metal trim, or as in a twist-em causes arcing. Never use a twist-em in the microwave oven. The wire in it can get so hot the paper covering can burst into flames.

The third thing that can happen to a microwave is that it can be *absorbed* by water molecules and converted to heat, as explained under *Heat Production*.

WHAT DOES "NO LOAD" MEAN?

For a microwave oven, a "no load" situation is when the oven is turned on empty or, even if something is in the oven, that something does not contain water molecules. If there are no water molecules to "absorb" the microwaves, the microwave pressure builds up in the oven. These waves can reflect back to the magnetron tube and damage or destroy it. Magnetron tubes are very expensive.

If your oven cannot take a "no load" situation, always keep a glass of water in it when it is not being used. Some ovens are better engineered and can take a "no load" situation better than other units. Check your operator's manual for the manufacturer's instructions for your unit. This is very important.

WHAT ABOUT RADIATION
   AND SAFETY?

Some of the most frequently asked questions are on safety and radiation. There are two types of radiation. One form is *nonionizing*. What this means is that if this form of radiation enters living cell tissue (you for instance), it will not cause chemical changes, it is not accumulative in its damages, and it cannot cause cancer. Non-ionizing radiation includes microwaves, ultra-high-frequency communication lines, radio, television, radar, infra-red, and light. Yes, light. Very few people realize that all light is radiation.

In fact, the only thing a microwave can do is produce heat in cell tissues just as they do in food. They would have to enter your body in large quantities to produce enough heat for you to even feel them. Microwaves lose power very quickly as they move away from the source that produces them. If a microwave oven could be made to work with the door opened wide, and if you stood 3 1/2 feet away from the oven, no microwaves would reach you. Of course, present ovens are designed so they *cannot* be operated with the door open.

The Federal Government regulates the safety standards for all microwave ovens sold in the United States. These standards are set by scientists working in the Department of Health, Education, and Welfare. These requirements are very strict.

The second form of radiation is *ionizing*. It does cause chemical changes in cell tissues, it is accumulative in its effect, and it can cause cancer. Ultraviolet rays, x-rays, gamma rays, and cosmic rays are ionizing rays. Some television sets are capable of generating a small amount of x-rays. Microwave ovens are not. The microwave oven is the safest single appliance made.

OTHER SAFETY FEATURES

The microwave oven is the safest appliance in the home. Check the records at any emergency hospital. There are many injuries involving all types of home appliances and equipment but not one involving a microwave oven. You cannot burn yourself on it. It cannot catch your clothes on fire. It won't catch the house on fire. It won't explode.

Due to the fact that microwave ovens have self-limiting cooking (the oven shuts itself off when the timer reaches 0.0), you can't forget and leave it turned on. Young children can heat foods in it at an early age, as soon as they can read and understand simple numbers.

Many microwave ovens have controls of a type that are difficult, if not impossible, for toddlers to operate. All microwave ovens turn off a split second before the door opens.

YOUR OBLIGATION TO SAFETY

Operate your oven according to the manufacturer's specifications. Keep your oven clean, especially around the door seals. Your oven operates better when it is clean. The greatest single cause of microwave leakage has been poor housekeeping.

Follow these simple safety regulations:

Never try to by-pass the interlocks or other safety mechanisms of your oven.

Never try to repair your unit yourself.

Never modify your oven.

Never remove the outer case. The microwave oven holds a tremendous electrical charge that needs to be grounded by a trained person so that it can be safely handled without the case. **15**

Never use metal in your oven if it cannot take metal. Remember, aluminum foil is metal. Containers with a ceramic finish and a teflon lining are usually metal.

Never use your oven in a "no load" situation if your oven cannot take it. (See *What Does "No Load" Mean?*)

PACEMAKERS

Ordinary pacemakers are not affected by microwave ovens but some "demand" type pacemakers can be inactivated or temporarily turned off by an operating microwave oven. Usually these are improperly shielded models. A person with this type of pacemaker can still use the oven safely. If you have a pacemaker of this type, walk to the oven, put in the food, start the oven, and walk at least 6 feet away. *Never* stay within 6 feet of an operating oven. If you need to approach an operating oven, do so quickly and immediately open the door. The microwave oven shuts off automatically if the door is opened. When the oven is shut off, it does not affect the pacemaker. If ever you are near an operating microwave oven and start to feel dizzy, move further away from the oven at once. And quickly.

HOW LONG DO MICROWAVES STAY
IN THE FOOD?

They don't. At night when a light is turned on, the room is lighted by the light rays. As soon as the switch turns off the electricity, the light ceases to exist. The same thing is true of microwaves. They exist only while the magnetron tube is turned on. Microwaves cannot be stored in the food any more than light rays can be stored in the room, or in the walls, or in anything else.

HOW TO COOK A T.V. DINNER

16 First, read the operator's manual that came with your microwave oven. If it says absolutely no metal may be used in your unit, take the food from the foil tray and put it in other containers. Cover the food and cook it until each food is done. Overall cooking time will be about 1 minute less than if cooking the food in the foil tray. This time saved in cooking is lost in transferring the food and in the time used for handling and washing the extra utensils. If your oven allows the use of small amounts of foil and the cooking of T.V. dinners in their own foil trays, take the tray out of its carton. Remove the top foil cover. Put the food back in the carton (the carton acts as a lid, holding in heat and steam), and put it in the microwave oven. Most dinners take about 7 minutes to cook. The larger sizes take longer.

Here are some problems that can occur. For the children's lunches that have a pudding in them, the pudding will not cook enough in the time needed to heat or cook the remaining food. Solution—take the pudding out while still frozen and put it in a custard dish. Cover it with plastic wrap or wax paper. Put it in the microwave oven first and cook until it is done. This allows it to cool a bit while the rest of the dinner is cooking.

Another problem occurs in T.V. dinners that have a corn bread, brownie, or other flour product included. These often overcook in the time needed to cook the other food. These can be removed from the tray and cooked separately, or you can check them from time-to-time to see when they are done and then cover them with a piece of foil to prevent further cooking while the remaining food cooks.

Still another problem occurs in a dinner containing fish or shrimp. Fish and shrimp cook faster than the remaining food and should be removed, or covered with foil, as soon as they are done. It is not possible to crisp foods in the microwave oven, so ignore any instructions that come with the dinner about covering or uncovering certain parts of the foods in the tray.

WHAT CONTAINERS
DO I COOK WITH?

Many types of containers can be used in the microwave oven; some surprise many people. Let's look at them one at a time.

Glass Heat-treated glass is best. You probably have casseroles and baking dishes of this material already. It comes most commonly under the trade names such as *Pyrex, Corning Ware,* and *Fire King.* Some of the pieces are clear glass and some opaque. Either are suitable. A few pieces may have decorations on them containing metal trim or paint with metal oxides in it. Test these trimmed pieces. Put some water in the container and turn the oven on. Check from time-to-time. If the trim gets hotter than the surrounding glass, it is best not to use it in the microwave oven, as it may crack.

China and Pottery The same thing is true of trim here, as in the glass above. Also, in some china and pottery there may be metal oxides in the clay or in the glazes. Use the same test as above. In addition, if the clay or glaze has metal oxides, the dish will heat faster than the water in it. If the water heats faster than the dish and if there is no trim that heats up, the piece is microwave-oven safe. If the serving pieces of your china set are safe, you can cook and serve in them, saving yourself some dishwashing.

Plastics There are two types of plastics. The soft or semi-soft moldable kind and melamine. You may know melamine as *Melmac.* Very often melamine plastics crack, warp, or blister in the microwave oven. Test your set by using the piece you least care about. Use it several times in the microwave oven. If nothing happens, probably the whole set is safe. More often than not, melamine cannot be used.

The other type of plastic will not crack or warp from the effect of the microwaves oven but great care must still be taken when using it. Microwaves do not generate heat in this type of plastic, but the plastic will pick up heat from the food and that can soften or warp it. If a piece of plastic can be used in the dishwasher, it may be used for light duty in the microwave oven. Use it for short-term cooking as in cooking vegetables or other light foods. Use it for short-term heating of foods as long as they do not contain a large amount of fat or sugar, or as long as the food is not too heavy or dense. Liquids may also be heated in Styrofoam cups.

Plastic Cooking Pouches and Bags Plastic browning bags that are made for conventional oven use may be used in the microwave oven, if you desire, but are really not needed. If you use one, never close it with a twist-em. There is a metal wire in it and the wire can get so hot the paper catches fire. Use a rubber band. It will not burn or smell bad in the microwave oven. Pouches that foods are sealed in can be used in the microwave oven safely with these precautions. Always put a slit in the top layer of the plastic as the bag lies in the microwave oven. This prevents the bag from bursting as steam pressure builds in it. Do not use plastic bags or pouches if the food contains a lot of fat or sugar, if the food is quite dense, or if the food must cook or heat for a long time, as the plastic can soften and rupture.

18

Paper or Cloth These materials are not affected by microwaves as they have no water molecules. They are transparent to microwaves and, as the oven has no heat of its own, will not catch fire in the microwave oven. One exception to this could be paper or cloth containing metal filaments. Do be careful about using recycled paper in the microwave oven as it could have some of these metal filaments. Bacon cooked on paper toweling atop a paper plate is the best way to cook bacon. All flour products, breads, rolls, sweet rolls, and such, should be wrapped in paper or cloth toweling or napkins to absorb the excess moisture that comes to the surface during heating. This prevents these foods from getting soggy.

Straw, Wood, Wicker, or Raffia Baskets of these materials may be used for heating breads or rolls. Wooden bowls and such may crack if used in the microwave oven for more than a minute or two because of moisture that may be in the wood.

Shell Shell is transparent to microwaves. It makes a nice cooking and serving piece for fish and shellfish dishes.

Metal Carefully read your operator's manual that came with your unit. If it says no metal, it means no metal. Some manuals are a bit contradictory. In one place it may say use no metal, yet in another it may say small amounts of foil can be used; or it may say that a T.V. dinner may be cooked in its own tray in the microwave oven. Metal containers, per se, may not be used in the microwave oven as microwaves cannot go through metal. This means that much of the efficiency of the oven is lost. Foods will overcook on top and undercook on the bottom. *If* your oven can use small amounts of metal, foil can be used to stop or slow down cooking of any part of the food that is cooking too fast or too much. Make certain the foil does not come too near any metal part or wall of the oven or arcing will occur and a permanent burn mark will be made on the metal part. This is true even of ovens that have an acrylic coating on the inside of the oven. *If* your oven can use metal, food may be cooked on metal skewers as long as the amount of food exceeds the amount of metal used. *If* your oven can use metal, a T.V. dinner may be cooked in its own tray. (For instructions see *How to Cook a T.V. Dinner.)*

19

ARE MICROWAVE OVENS
SELF-CLEANING?

Portable microwave ovens are not self-cleaning. Because the oven has no heat of its own and does not get very hot, food spills, boil-overs, and spatters do not burn onto the finish. Most things wipe up with a damp sponge, paper towel, or dishcloth. Even the most dehydrated spill only needs 10 or 20 seconds of soaking time and it will wipe up. It is necessary to keep the oven clean though, as spills can alter the heat-distribution pattern. Food spills, if allowed to build up in the door-seal area, could conceivably cause minor microwave leakage.

TURNING (ROTATING)
AND TURNING OVER

These two terms mean two different things but are both used to obtain even cooking. Some ovens, especially older models, do not have a good heat-distribution pattern. Directions in the cookbooks that come with the oven say to give the food a quarter or half turn every so often. This is because there are hot and cold spots in the oven and turning the food evens out the cooking. Even in ovens with a good heat-distribution pattern it may occasionally be better to turn certain foods. Sometimes the food itself causes the heat-distribution pattern to change. Foods that have fat, sugar, or bone that are not evenly distributed in them will cause the pattern to warp. One make of oven has a carousel in it to automatically move the food through the hot and cold spots.

Foods often cook and brown more quickly from the bottom than the top. This is because the food is closer to the bottom wall of the oven than the top wall. All dense foods should be *turned over* at least once during the cooking period to even out the cooking from top to bottom. This turning over also shortens the cooking time. Dense foods that should be turned over are: chickens, turkeys, roasts, whole potatoes, whole sweet potatoes or yams, and whole hard squashes. Large turkeys should not only be turned over several times during the cooking period but should also be reversed in the microwave oven several times. This means to put the breast-side in first for part of the cooking time and the tail-end in first for the other part of the cooking time.

20

COOKING TIME FACTORS

Three things have a major influence on the microwave oven cooking times. Other factors have lesser influence. These items also affect cooking time in conventional cooking but are not readily noticed as one does not cook by "timing" in conventional cooking.

These major influences are as follows:

Starting temperature influences total cooking time. The colder a food is, the longer it must cook.

The *density* of the food affects its cooking time. A light-weight, porous food will cook much faster than a dense, solid food. Notice how much quicker a roll will cook in relationship to a potato. The roll, being light-weight and porous, cooks much faster than the dense potato.

The *total amount of food* cooking in the oven at a single time affects the cooking time more than any other thing. Two slices of bacon cook in about 2 minutes. Four slices of bacon take almost four minutes. There is no firm, fast rule about how to increase the cooking time when increasing the amount of food, but it is wise to allow double the cooking time when the food is doubled.

Other things have less influence on cooking times but are still very important. They can shorten or lengthen the cooking time.

First is the choice of cooking container. Some containers are more transparent to microwaves than others and let the microwaves through better. *Centura Ware* by Corning should never be used in cooking as it is, at best, translucent to microwaves.

The shape of the cooking container affects cooking times. A large, shallow container will cook the same amount of food faster than a deeper container of the same capacity. This is because the shallow container exposes more surface area of the food to microwaves.

The more surface area of the food that is exposed to the microwaves, the more heat can be generated and the quicker the food will cook.

Stirring will also shorten the cooking time. Heat is generated in the outer layers of the food and then must reach the center by conduction. Conduction is a slow way for heat to travel through food. By stirring, cold food from the center of the food mass is brought to the surface to be heated and hot food from the surface is taken to the center. This evens out the heat. **21**

In some ovens, turning the food evens out the cooking by turning the food through hot and cold areas of the oven.

ABOUT BROWNING

Realistically, most foods that cook for less than 15 minutes in the microwave oven will have little or no browning. An exception is bacon. Bacon browns beautifully. Most foods that cook for more than 15 minutes usually brown. There are many aids to use to make foods brown or at least to appear browner. There are browning trays, built-in browners, and browning aids such as dry gravy mix, spice mixtures, Worcestershire Sauce, and Kitchen Bouquet. Breads, cakes, pies, and cookies normally do not brown in the microwave oven.

SCHEDULING OF COOKING

Many people ask, "Can I cook more than one thing at a time?" It takes just as long to cook two things together as it does to cook each one separately and it is easier to judge cooking times if each one is cooked separately. The important thing is to know what to cook in what order so that all dishes will come out hot and done at the same time.

The food that takes the longest to cook should be cooked first because it will hold its heat the longest. The food that takes the second longest to cook will start losing its heat just a little sooner. The food that cooks the fastest will start losing heat the quickest so should be cooked last. If this sequence is followed, all dishes will be ready to eat at once.

WHEN AND WHAT FOODS
SHOULD BE COVERED

22 All foods that can take moist heat should be covered. Covering holds in the heat and steam generated by the microwaves in the food. If food is not covered, some of this heat and steam escapes to heat up the inside of the oven and some of the oven efficiency is reduced. If a baking dish has its own lid, use it. If it does not, use wax paper or plastic wrap as a cover. Wax paper diffuses microwaves more evenly. Plastic wrap will give a tighter fitting cover when that is needed.

WHAT CAN A MICROWAVE
OVEN DO?

A microwave oven is designed to do three jobs. First of all, it can do primary cooking. Second of all, it can reheat foods. Thirdly, it can defrost frozen foods.

MUST FROZEN FOODS BE DEFROSTED?

Yes. Microwaves react many times faster on water in the liquid state than they do on that in the frozen state. If you tried to cook something without defrosting it first, it might appear done on the outside but be cool, cold, or even partly frozen inside. The exception to this is small packages of frozen vegetables.

MICROWAVE LIMITATIONS

Microwaves cannot cook:
eggs in the shell
popovers
cream puffs and eclairs
angel food cakes
true soufflés
raw pizza

Microwaves cannot:
make toast
do true broiling
do deep fat frying
crisp foods
bake foods that need to be
cooked on a hot surface

23

HOW TO ARRANGE FOOD

Food cooks more quickly at the outer edge of the container. Food cooks more slowly in the center of a dish or food grouping. Put the largest, densest, or thickest part of any piece of food to the outer edge. Put thinner, smaller, or less dense pieces in the center. This evens out the cooking of irregularly shaped pieces of food. Regularly shaped foods should be arranged in a hollow circle when possible. If not possible, rearrange pieces from time-to-time. Irregularly shaped potatoes are best arranged spoke fashion with the smaller end toward the middle and the large end out. When cooking a single potato choose those most uniformly shaped for even cooking. When reheating mixed foods on a plate, put the less dense foods in the plate's center and the denser foods around the plate's edge.

REHYDRATION—HUH?

Rehydration is a very special type of cooking. Literally it means putting water back into a dry food. It is the one form of cooking that is not greatly speeded up in the microwave oven. This includes the cooking of rice, pastas, and dried beans, peas, and lentils. The advantage of cooking these foods in the microwave oven is that they do not scorch, stick, or burn.

SEASONINGS

All seasoning is done in the same manner as in conventional cooking with one exception. That is salt. Salt is best added after or near the end of the cooking cycle. Salt has an osmotic effect on foods, that is, it pulls water out of foods and tends to toughen them. This is especially true of carrots.

24 CAN I STACK FOODS?

Not in most counter top microwave ovens, as only the top of the upper layer of food and the bottom of the lower layer would cook. Exception—"whole meal" ovens.

REHEATING

Foods reheated in the microwave oven taste fresh-cooked. Leftovers never taste like leftovers.

WHY AREN'T THERE SHELVES IN MOST MICROWAVE OVEN?

This is because foods would then be stacked one over the other and neither layer of food would cook properly. There is one type of oven, though, that is especially designed for the use of a metal rack as well as the ceramic shelf.

WATTAGES AND COOKING TIMES

Most recipes and cookbooks are written for units emitting 600 to 650 watts of power. If your oven takes 500 to 550 watts, add 10 percent cooking time. If your oven is around 400 to 450 watts, add 20 percent cooking time. Exact cooking times cannot be given in recipes because there are too many variables. Cooking times given are always the least possible time in which foods can cook. Do not be surprised if you have to add more cooking time for your unit. The shortest possible cooking times are given because it is always possible to add more cooking time but it is impossible to uncook what is already overcooked.

FLOUR PRODUCTS

Cakes do not brown in the microwave oven. Cook them only until they lose that wet, glossy appearance. Cakes rise higher in the microwave oven and are more moist.

Single-crust pies may be cooked entirely in the microwave oven. Cook the crust first and then add the cooked or uncooked filling. If uncooked filling is being used, it is cooked in the precooked pie shell. A two-crust pie may be started in the microwave oven. Cook it only until the juice begins to bubble through the steam vents. Finish off in a very hot conventional oven to set and brown the crust.

Breads neither brown nor crust. If browning and crusting are an integral part of baking the bread, it must be baked conventionally. Bread used for toast or sandwiches may be baked in the microwave oven.

Most cookies are best done conventionally. Cookies need a hot surface to bake on to achieve their crispness and texture. There is no hot surface in the microwave oven. Bar cookies, however, are often satisfactory in the microwave oven.

When baking cup cakes, each one will take a slightly different amount of baking due to slightly differing amounts of batter.

STANDING TIME

This is the time needed in many foods between the point at which they are taken from the cooking unit and the point at which they are served. This time is needed to allow residual cooking to take place. The heavier and denser a food, the more standing time is needed.

MEATS, FISH, AND POULTRY

26

Meat, fish, and poultry have less shrinkage and are more moist and more juicy than those cooked conventionally. There will be less browning and crusting. The nutrition will be the same. Tougher cuts of meat can be cooked in the microwave oven only if there is a slow simmer type of cooking speed available.

VEGETABLES AND FRUITS

Vegetables and fruits retain more of their fresh color and fresh taste than in conventional cooking. They usually retain more nutrients also. For fresh vegetables, most are cooked in their own steam. Dryer vegetables need only about 1/4 cup of water added. Frozen vegetables, except lima beans, need no added water. Canned vegetables are already cooked and need only be heated. More vitamin C and other heat-sensitive nutrients are retained in microwave cooking. Undercook vegetables slightly to allow for the residual cooking.

COOKING WITH VARIABLE POWER SETTINGS

Being able to choose the power you use in your microwave oven gives you the same end results as being able to choose the temperature you want in your conventional range. Many times using a lower power will give you much better results in the quality of the food you prepare in the microwave oven. Also, being able to choose a lower power will allow you to "simmer" those foods that need it.

Most vegetables do not need a lower power for cooking, that is if they are not being cooked along with some heat-sensitive food. When a heat-sensitive food is added to the vegetable, then a lower power setting is very desirable.

Most of the sauces that are thickened with flour, cornstarch, or arrow root powder will come to a boil before the starch in these products has time to cook through. As a result, sometimes the sauces do not thicken properly and they have a raw flour taste. To counteract these effects, it is necessary to cook the sauce longer. If lower powers are available, it is possible to cook slowly for 2 or 3 minutes at the simmer. If these powers are not available, then the sauce should be allowed to stand for 2 minutes and then cooked 1 minute more on high (the only power then available). Some residual cooking will take place during that 2 minutes standing time. The final minute of cooking will finish the cooking process.

If your oven is a single-powered oven, you have no choice of powers. Your single power is cook or high. Following the instructions for allowing 2 minutes of standing time and then cooking for 1 minute longer, you should be able to achieve a very good sauce.

Your oven has two powers if it has cook and defrost settings. The defrost is usually half power or 50 percent of full power. Two minutes of cooking at the defrost setting should be adequate.

Your oven has three powers if it has cook, defrost, and slow cook. Use the lowest setting and cook the sauces about 3 minutes on that setting.

If you have four or more powers, the sauce should be cooked on the setting that approximates 30 percent power or a third of full power.

To find out what setting on your oven equals half and third powers, use a measuring cup-full of tap water. Heat it in your microwave oven for 3 minutes. The setting that will raise the water temperature by 65 degrees will give you half power. The setting that will raise the water temperature by 45 degrees will give you third power.

If your oven has settings, or divisions, numbered from 1 to 10, or 1 to 9 plus cook or high, then setting number 5 should give half power and setting number 3 should give third power.

28

COOKING VEGETABLES
BY CONVENTIONAL METHODS

All the times and methods given in the recipes in the body of this book are geared to microwave cooking. Any experienced cook could look at the recipes and convert them to conventional cooking easily.

Any of the sauces may be made in a saucepan on the stove top burners. Cook over low heat and stir constantly until the mixture comes to a boil. The one exception is the Hollandaise Sauce. Find a conventional recipe in a good cookbook and follow it.

The best methods for cooking vegetables conventionally are steaming and waterless cooking. Both methods conserve all possible nutrients and flavor. In steaming, the vegetables are held in a basket over boiling water and cooked in the steam until they are tender. In waterless cooking, the vegetables are cooked in a heavy saucepan with a tight-fitting lid without any water other than that which clings to the vegetables after washing. It is necessary to cook over very low heat so that the produce does not scorch.

29

Try this test and you will be convinced that waterless cooking is well worth the effort. Cook equal amounts of carrots in two saucepans. In one, cover the carrots with water. In the other, use the waterless cooking method. Compare the flavors. Look at the color of the water being discarded. That color is flavor and nutrition.

Some people like artichokes cooked in boiling water until tender. This would be the only vegetable that should be cooked in water. Even artichokes can be cooked waterless, though.

One of the best ways to cook asparagus or broccoli, conventionally, is to stand it up in a coffee pot. Have the butt ends standing in 3 inches of boiling water. The boiling water cooks the butt ends at about the same rate the steam cooks the tender tops.

When a recipe calls for onion cooked in butter in the microwave oven, cook it in a saucepan over low heat until the onions are tender but not browned.

As in microwave cooking, judge cooking time by the tenderness of the vegetables. If you are a person just learning to cook, don't hesitate to taste and chew a piece of the vegetable. Is it tender?

Does it still have texture? Does it have a cooked taste? If the answers are yes, consider it done. As you acquire more experience, you will be able to judge doneness by pricking with a fork.

Bread crumbs, for toppings, may be toasted in a heavy skillet on the stove top burner. They will need almost constant stirring to prevent scorching. Prepare a quantity at one time. Store in the freezer until needed.

Most recipes should be done entirely on the stove top burners. A few will need to be partially cooked in the conventional oven.

Broil only
   Broiled Tomatoes Parmesan

Bake only
   Carrot Pudding
   Roast Dripping Potatoes
   Stuffed Tomatoes
   Rice-Stuffed Tomatoes

Complete the Cooking by Baking
   Gratinée of Artichoke
   Asparagus with Swiss Cheese, and Tomato Sauce
   Avocado-Tomato Bake
   Baked Avocado Supreme
   Avocado, Cheese, and Bacon Bake
   Green Beans Supreme
   Greek Style Baked Beans
   Noni's Broccoli-Rice Bake
   Carrot Gold
   Cauliflower and Eggplant in Parmesan Sauce
   Baked Eggplant with Cheese and Tomatoes
   Eggplant with Dried-Fruit Stuffing
   Spinach and Rice Casserole
   Jerusalem Artichokes En Casserole
   Leek Dish From Vaud
   Chinese Stuffed Mushrooms
   Finnish Baked Mushrooms
   Baked Stuffed Onions
   Summer Squash Casserole
   Squash Pudding
   Stuffed Acorn Squash
   Snow-Capped Yams
   Yam-Stuffed Bananas
   Sherried Turnip Casserole

COMPARISON OF COOKING TIMES

First of all, in checking microwave cooking times against boiling time, remember that the timing of the cooking period starts *after* the water comes to a boil. The microwave cooking times are from the instant the oven is turned on. If you choose to steam or water-less cook your vegetables, depending on the density, you will need from 5 to 15 minutes longer cooking times than the times shown for boiling.

Vegetable	Amount	Microwave (minutes)	Conventional Boiling (minutes)
Artichoke	4 large	20	45
Asparagus	1 pound	7–10	10–20
Beets	2 bunches	15–30	30–45
Broccoli	1½ lbs.	7–12	10–15
Brussels Sprouts	1½ lbs.	9–10	10
Cabbage	1½ lbs.	9–10	10–15
Carrots	1 lb.	7–10	15–20
Cauliflower	1 head	6–10	20–30
Celery	3 cups	10	10–20
Corn	4 ears	7–10	8–10
Eggplant	1 medium	5–9	10–15
Green Beans	1 lb.	12–15	15–20
Green Peppers	1 lb.	7	10
Jerusalem Artichoke	1 lb.	7	10–15
Leeks	1½ lbs.	7–8	10–15
Lima Beans (fresh)	1 lb.	20–30	20–30
Mushrooms (fried)	½ lb.	10–12	8–10
Okra	½ lb.	5–6	10–15
Onions	4 large	7–9	30–35
Parsnips	1 lb.	7–10	25–30
Peas (green)	2 cups	7–8	8–12
Potatoes	1½ lbs.	15	30–40
Spinach	2 lbs.	6–8	8–10
Squash (summer)	1½ lbs.	8–9	10–15
Squash (winter)	1½ lbs.	9–10	30–60
Sweet Potatoes	1½ lbs.	10–12	30–40
Tomatoes	1 lb.	3	8–10
Turnips	1½ lbs.	12	20–30

FRESH VEGETABLE BUYING CALENDAR

Due to modern agricultural practices, many vegetables are available the year around, or nearly so. Usually the months of greatest availability are the months of better quality and lower prices. Availability will vary with the locale you live in.

32

	January	February	March	April	May	June	July	August	September	October	November	December
Artichoke		•	•	•	•							
Asparagus			•	•	•	•						
Beets	•	•	•	•	•							
Broccoli		•	•	•						•	•	•
Brussels Sprouts	•	•	•							•	•	•
Cabbage	•	•	•		•		•	•	•	•	•	
Carrots			•	•	•	•	•			•	•	•
Cauliflower	•	•	•	•						•	•	
Celery	•	•	•		•	•	•	•			•	•
Corn						•	•	•	•	•		
Eggplant							•	•	•	•		
Green Beans						•	•	•	•	•		
Green Peppers						•	•	•	•	•		
Jerusalem Artichokes	•									•	•	•
Leeks						•		•	•	•	•	•
Lima Beans (fresh)							•	•	•	•		
Mushrooms	•	•	•	•							•	•
Okra							•	•		•		
Onions					•	•	•	•	•			
Parsnips	•									•	•	•
Peas (green)				•	•				•	•	•	
Potatoes	•	•	•		•	•	•	•		•	•	
Spinach			•	•	•	•						•
Squash (summer)							•	•	•	•		
Squash (winter)										•	•	•
Sweet Potatoes										•	•	•
Tomatoes					•	•	•	•	•	•		
Turnips & Rutabagas	•	•	•						•	•	•	•

SAUCES

What's sauce for the goose is sauce for the gander. What is good with one vegetable is often good with another. So, instead of putting the recipe for a sauce in with any one vegetable, the sauce recipes have been grouped in this chapter. Most vegetable chapters will have suggestions for sauces that are suitable with that vegetable.

Often a good restaurant, especially a French restaurant, will have a saucier, a person who does nothing but make sauces. A sauce can change a dish from blah to hurrah.

Making a sauce in the microwave oven is super easy. There is no chance of burning, scorching, or sticking, and one does not have to stand over a hot range stirring constantly. Most sauces are stirred 2 or 3 times during the cooking period plus once more as soon as the cooking is completed. No stirring is needed until the liquid starts to warm up. If you forget to stir, the starch will go out of solution, settle to the bottom, and form a thick gummy layer at the bottom of the liquid. The starch is the flour, cornstarch, or arrowroot powder that is used to thicken the liquid.

Let the timer on your microwave oven help you remember to stir the sauce. Instead of setting the timer for the total time needed for the sauce, set it for when the stirring should take place. On recipes that make 1 cup of sauce, set the timer for 1 minute, stir, set the timer for another minute, stir. Finish the cooking and stir once more. For 2 cups of sauce, plan to stir at the end of every 1½-minute period.

In the microwave oven, a sauce will come to a boil so quickly that the flour (or other thickening agent) will not have time to cook properly. It will not thicken well and the flour will have a "raw" taste. It is necessary to cook the sauce a bit longer and, if your oven has lower powers, it is best to do this additional cooking on defrost or low. Two or three minutes will be enough. If these powers are not available, let the sauce sit for 2 minutes and then cook 1 minute more on high. Notice how much better the sauce is thickened and how much better the flavor is.

Please your family with a Béchamel, Mornay, or Orange sauce made easily in just a few minutes in your microwave oven. Once you've done sauces in your microwave oven, you will never go back to doing them conventionally.

	White	Cheese	Velouté	Allemande	Béchamel	Bearnaise	Mornay	Parsley	Tomato Provençal	Garlic	Hollandaise	Butter and Seed	Hot Poppy Seed	Hot Orange
Artichokes				•		•		•	•				•	
Asparagus		•	•	•	•	•	•	•	•	•	•	•	•	•
Avocado					•									
Bean Sprouts			•		•	•		•		•		•	•	•
Beets	•				•			•	•					
Broccoli		•	•	•	•	•		•	•		•	•	•	•
Brussels Sprouts		•	•	•				•		•	•	•	•	•
Cabbage		•	•			•	•	•		•	•	•	•	•
Carrots	•	•	•	•					•	•	•	•		•
Cauliflower		•	•	•		•	•	•		•	•	•	•	•
Celeriac					•	•	•	•	•	•	•	•	•	•
Celery					•	•	•	•	•	•	•	•	•	•
Corn						•								
Edible Pod Peas						•	•			•		•		•
Eggplant		•			•	•					•			
Green Beans			•			•		•	•	•	•			
Green Peppers						•								
Greens		•	•	•	•	•		•	•		•		•	
Jerusalem Artichokes				•		•		•	•					•
Leeks		•	•	•		•	•	•		•	•		•	
Lentils						•							•	
Lima Beans			•			•		•	•	•	•			
Mushrooms		•					•	•	•	•	•			
Okra						•								
Onions		•	•	•		•	•	•	•	•	•	•	•	•
Parsnips		•	•			•								
Peas		•	•	•				•		•	•	•		•
Potatoes							•	•		•		•	•	•
Rutabagas		•		•		•	•	•			•		•	
Spinach				•						•		•		•
Squash (summer)		•	•	•	•	•	•	•	•		•		•	
Squash (winter)	•													
Sweet Potatoes	•													
Tomatoes						•								
Turnips		•		•		•	•	•			•		•	
Yams	•													

WHITE SAUCE

White sauce is the old standby. While it has often been overused, it is still a very good sauce. Adding wine and mustard will take it out of the ordinary. Try adding a dash of other herbs to find out which ones are for you.

Makes about 1 cup *Preparation time 7 Min.*

2 tablespoons butter or margarine	1/4 teaspoon dry mustard (optional)
2 tablespoons flour	1 cup milk or cream
1/2 teaspoon salt	2 tablespoons dry white wine (optional)
White pepper to taste	

Melt the butter in a 2-cup measure or small casserole in the microwave oven. (This will take about 45 to 60 seconds.) Stir in, until smooth, the flour, salt, pepper, and mustard. Blend in the milk or cream and the wine. Cook in the microwave oven, stirring several times, until the sauce thickens and boils. (This will take about 3 to 3 1/2 minutes.) Continue cooking for 2 or 3 minutes more on defrost or low power. If these powers are not available, let the sauce sit for 2 minutes and then cook 1 minute more on high.

35

Tip: to make a thinner sauce, use only 1 tablespoon each of the butter and flour. To make a thicker sauce, use 3 tablespoons each of the butter and flour. In making sauces, gravies, or puddings in the microwave oven, it is not necessary to stir until the liquid starts to get warm. Constant stirring is not needed.

My Time Is _____ Min.

It is hard to think of Brussels sprouts without thinking of Cheese sauce; yet there are so many uses for this delectably-flavored sauce. Its flavor can be varied by the type and amount of cheese that is added.

Makes 1 1/2 cups

- 2 tablespoons butter or margarine
- 2 tablespoons flour
- 1/2 teaspoon salt
  White pepper to taste
- 1/4 teaspoon dry mustard (optional)

Preparation time 8 Min.

- 1 cup milk or cream
- 2 tablespoons dry white wine (optional)
- 1/2 cup (or more) grated cheese such as American, Cheddar, Swiss, or Gruyère.

36 Melt the butter in a 2-cup measure or small casserole in the microwave oven. (This will take about 45 to 60 seconds.) Stir in, until smooth, the flour, salt, pepper, and mustard. Blend in the milk or cream and the wine. Cook in the microwave oven, stirring several times, until the sauce thickens and boils. (This will take about 3 to 3 1/2 minutes.) Continue cooking for 2 or 3 minutes more on defrost or low power. If these powers are not available, let the sauce sit for 2 minutes and then cook 1 minute more on high. Add the cheese and stir until it melts and the sauce is smooth. Reheat 30 to 60 seconds but do not allow the sauce to boil.

Tip: this sauce will lose quality if it is allowed to boil or heat too long after adding the cheese. If you have multiple powers on your oven, use a low power and heat a little longer.

My Time Is _____ Min.

VELOUTÉ (VELVET) SAUCE

Velouté or Velvet sauce is similar to White sauce except that a broth is used as the liquid. Chicken broth is usually used. To make it easier for you, this recipe uses chicken bouillon concentrate. If you use the broth, use 1 cup broth in place of the water and delete the chicken bouillon concentrate.

Makes about 1 cup   *Preparation time 7 Min.*

2 tablespoons butter or margarine

2 tablespoons flour

1 teaspoon chicken bouillon concentrate

1/4 teaspoon salt

Dash of pepper

Dash of nutmeg (optional)

1 cup water

Melt the butter in a 2-cup measure or a small casserole in the microwave oven. (This will take 45 to 60 seconds.) Stir in, until smooth, the flour, chicken bouillon concentrate, salt, pepper, and nutmeg. Blend in the water. Cook in the microwave oven, stirring occasionally, until the sauce thickens and boils. (This will take about 3 to 3 1/2 minutes.) Continue cooking for 2 or 3 minutes more on defrost or low power. If these powers are not available, let the sauce sit for 2 minutes and then cook 1 minute more on **37** high.

Tip: for a variation, replace the salt with celery salt. On other occasions, cook 1 teaspoon each of finely-minced celery, onion, and mushroom in the butter for 2 minutes before adding the remaining ingredients.

My Time Is _____ Min.

BÉCHAMEL SAUCE

Béchamel sauce was named after Louis de Béchamel, a steward to King Louis XIV of France. This sauce uses as a base both cream (milk) and chicken bouillon. The following recipe is very easy and tasty.

Makes about 1 cup   *Preparation time 7 Min.*

2 tablespoons butter or margarine	Dash of pepper
2 tablespoons flour	1/4 teaspoon onion powder (or 1 teaspoon finely-minced onion)
1/2 teaspoon chicken bouillon concentrate	1/8 teaspoon nutmeg
1/4 teaspoon salt	1 cup milk or cream

Melt the butter in a 2-cup measure or a small casserole in the microwave oven. (This should take about 45 to 60 seconds.) Stir in, until smooth, the flour, bouillon concentrate, salt, pepper, onion powder (or onion), and nutmeg. Blend in the milk or cream. Cook in the microwave oven, stirring several times, until the sauce thickens and boils. (This will take 3 to 3 1/2 minutes.) Continue cooking for 2 or 3 minutes more on defrost or low power. If these powers are not available, let the sauce sit for 2 minutes and then cook 1 minute more on high.

38

Tip: cream makes a richer, smoother sauce but has more calories. If you are watching calories, use milk. If you are dieting, use skimmed milk and only 1 tablespoon of the butter. Stirring is not needed until the liquid starts to warm.

ALLEMANDE SAUCE

Allemande sauce is a bit sharper in taste than the Velouté (Velvet) sauce. It goes well with cabbage, Brussels sprouts, celeriac, and other vegetables whose flavor can stand the robust taste of this sauce.

Makes 1 cup

2 tablespoons butter
2 tablespoons flour
1 teaspoon chicken bouillon concentrate
1 cup water

Preparation time 8 Min.

Salt and pepper to taste
1 beaten egg yolk
1 teaspoon lemon juice
2 teaspoons cream

Melt the butter in a 2-cup measure or a small casserole in the microwave oven. (This should take about 45 seconds.) Blend in the flour and the chicken bouillon concentrate. Gradually stir in the water. Add the salt and pepper. Cook in the microwave oven, stirring after each minute of cooking, until the mixture comes to a boil. Continue cooking for 2 or 3 minutes more on defrost or low power. If these powers are not available, let the sauce sit for 2 minutes and then cook 1 minute more on high. Stir a bit of the hot mixture into the egg yolk, then stir the egg yolk into the remaining hot sauce. Stir in the lemon juice and then the cream. Reheat about 30 seconds but do not let boil or the sauce will curdle.

39

Tip: a touch of powdered mustard would add even more zest to this sauce. You might even like a bit of caraway seed added when it is used with some vegetables.

My Time Is _____ Min.

BEARNAISE SAUCE

This is not quite a true Bearnaise sauce as it contains only 1/2 to 1/4 the amount of vinegar usually used in that sauce. With this variation, it becomes a sauce for many of the stronger flavored vegetables. True Bearnaise sauce is usually served with meats, but this version will make green beans or cabbage sing with flavor.

Makes about 1 cup   *Preparation time 4 Min.*

1 tablespoon chopped shallot or green onion	Dash of pepper
	Dash of cayenne (optional)
2 teaspoons minced, fresh or 1/2 teaspoon dried tarragon	1 tablespoon wine vinegar
	1/4 cup dry white wine
	1/2 cup butter or margarine
1/4 teaspoon salt	4 egg yolks

40 Mix all the ingredients, except the egg yolks, in a cup measure and heat about 2 minutes in the microwave oven until the butter melts. Do not allow it to get too hot. Beat the egg yolks in a small casserole. Gradually beat in the warm butter mixture. Start cooking for 10-second intervals, stirring well after each interval, until the sauce thickens. (This will take about 1 to 1 1/2 minutes.)

Tip: do not let the sauce get too hot or it will curdle. This sauce is not traditionally served piping hot, but rather lukewarm. If the vegetables are hot when the sauce is added, they will heat the sauce through.

My Time Is _____ Min.

MORNAY SAUCE

Mornay sauce is a cheese sauce made with both milk and chicken bouillon. The bouillon and mustard give it a distinctive flavor. It is a very elegant addition to vegetables.

Makes about 2 cups　　　　　　　*Preparation time 10 Min.*

- 2 tablespoons butter or margarine
- 2 tablespoons flour
- 1/4 teaspoon salt
- Dash of pepper
- 1/2 teaspoon chicken bouillon concentrate

- 1/2 teaspoon prepared Dijon-type mustard
- 1 1/2 cups milk or cream
- 1/4 cup grated Parmesan cheese
- 1/2 cup grated Swiss or Gruyère cheese

Melt the butter in a 2-cup measure or a small casserole in the microwave oven. (This should take about 45 to 60 seconds.) Stir in, until smooth, the flour, salt, pepper, bouillon concentrate, and mustard. Blend in the milk or cream. Cook in the microwave oven stirring several times until the sauce thickens and boils. (This will take about 5 minutes.) Continue cooking for 2 or 3 minutes more on defrost or low power. If these powers are not available, let the sauce sit for 2 minutes and then cook 1 minute more on **41** high. Stir in the cheese. Continue stirring until the cheese melts and the sauce is smooth. Reheat a bit if necessary, but do not allow sauce to boil.

Tip: stirring is not needed until the liquid starts to warm. This is usually about 2 1/2 minutes after the oven starts. It is a good idea to set the timer for this amount of time as a reminder to start stirring at this point. Constant stirring is not necessary in microwave cooking of sauces.

My Time Is _____ Min.

PARSLEY SAUCE

Parsley sauce is especially nice with carrots or any other vegetables which provide color contrast as well as complementary flavor. Excellent with potatoes.

Makes about 1 cup *Preparation time 8 Min.*

2 tablespoons butter or margarine	Pepper to taste
2 tablespoons flour	Dash of nutmeg
1 teaspoon chicken bouillon concentrate	1 cup water
1/4 teaspoon salt	2 egg yolks
	1/4 cup finely-chopped fresh parsley

42 Melt the butter in a 2-cup measure or a small casserole in the microwave oven. (This will take about 45 to 60 seconds.) Stir in the flour, chicken bouillon concentrate, salt, pepper, and nutmeg. Blend in the water until smooth. Cook in the microwave oven, stirring several times, until the sauce thickens and boils. (This will take about 3 to 3 1/2 minutes.) Continue cooking for 2 or 3 minutes more on defrost or low power. If these powers are not available, let the sauce sit for 2 minutes and then cook 1 minute more on high. Beat the egg yolks in a small dish. Blend in some of the hot sauce, 1 teaspoon at a time. Quickly blend the egg mixture into the remaining sauce. Stir in the parsley.

Tip: if a little more "zing" is desired in the flavor of this sauce, leave out the nutmeg and add a dash or two of either bottled hot pepper sauce or cayenne pepper.

My Time Is _____ Min.

TOMATO SAUCE PROVENÇAL

This is a hearty, robust sauce that will go equally well with both vegetables and protein dishes. Since it makes up a quart, the remaining part may be frozen and used later.

Makes 4 cups   *Preparation time 45 Min.*

- 1 cup dry red wine
- 1 can (8 ounces) tomato sauce
- 1 cup beef bouillon
- 1 teaspoon wine vinegar
- 2 cloves garlic, minced
- 1 cup chopped onion
- 1/2 cup chopped carrot
- 1/2 cup chopped green pepper
- 1/4 cup chopped parsley
- 1 cup chopped mushrooms
- 1/4 teaspoon dried thyme leaves
- 1/2 teaspoon dried basil leaves
- 1 bay leaf
   Salt and pepper to taste

Put all the ingredients in a large, covered casserole. Cook, covered, in the microwave oven, stirring occasionally, for 40 minutes. Remove the cover and continue cooking until the sauce is thick, stirring occasionally, if needed.

43

Tip: after trying the recipe once, if you wish to make it in bulk, double or triple the amounts. Naturally, more cooking time will be needed. Bring the mixture to a boil and cook, covered, until the vegetables are well cooked. Remove the lid and cook until the sauce is thick. This is an all-purpose sauce and may be used often.

My Time Is _____ Min.

GARLIC SAUCE

This zesty sauce is reminiscent of Italy and Greece where good cooks are not afraid to use garlic liberally when it adds to the gusto and enjoyment of a dish. This sauce is not for those who abhor garlic.

Makes 1/2 cup
- 2 tablespoons butter
- 2 cloves garlic, minced
  Dash of cayenne

Preparation time 4 Min.
Salt and pepper to taste
1/2 cup mayonnaise

Put the butter, garlic, cayenne, salt, and pepper in a small dish in the microwave oven and cook for 1 minute. Slowly beat into the mayonnaise.

Tip: serve this over green beans with a tablespoon of almond slices. For a change of pace, add 1/2 teaspoon powdered mustard and try it with cabbage.

44

My Time Is _____ Min.

HOLLANDAISE SAUCE

Hollandaise sauce is really butter thickened with egg yolk and lightly seasoned with lemon juice and cayenne. It is the richest of all sauces and should be used in small amounts.

Makes about 1/2 cup

A pinch of salt
Pepper to taste (white
  pepper preferred)
Dash or two of cayenne
A few drops of lemon
  juice

Preparation time 4 Min.

1/4 pound butter (1 stick)
4 egg yolks
1 tablespoon light cream
  (half and half)

Put the salt, pepper, cayenne, lemon juice, and butter in a small mixing bowl. Microwave 30 seconds. Stir the butter to distribute the heat evenly. Microwave about 15 seconds more or until the last of the butter is almost melted. Beat until smooth. Add the egg yolks and cream. Beat until well blended. Microwave 15 seconds; beat well. Microwave 15 seconds; beat well. Continue this pattern until the mixture thickens. (This will not take long.) If the mixture should curdle, add a few more drops of the cream and beat vigorously until smooth.

45

If your oven does not have a timer that reads in seconds, use the sweep hand of the kitchen clock, if you have one, or slowly count out the seconds.

Tip: beating hard with a wisk or egg beater is the secret of un-curdling the sauce. Though this recipe takes a small amount of vigorous beating, it takes much less beating than making the sauce conventionally would.

My Time Is _____ Min.

BUTTER AND SEED SAUCE

This is a modified form of Hollandaise sauce; it will not be as thick as the traditional form. Any seed that will complement the flavor of a vegetable can be used. The sauce may be made ahead of time and then chilled in the refrigerator. If it is chilled, stir it well before the sauce sets too firmly so the seed won't all be at the bottom of the sauce. This way, just what is needed can be taken out and stirred into hot, well drained, vegetables.

Makes a scant 1/2 cup
- 1/4 cup butter or margarine
- Salt and pepper to taste
- 1 teaspoon lemon juice
- 1 teaspoon seed (poppy, sesame, caraway, etc.)

Preparation time 3 Min.
- 1 egg yolk
- 1 tablespoon light cream (half and half)

Put the butter, salt, pepper, lemon juice, and seed in a small bowl and heat in the microwave oven until the butter comes to a boil. Meanwhile, beat the egg yolk and cream together until smooth. Then slowly beat the butter mixture into the sauce. The sauce will be smooth and thicken slightly.

46

Tip: adding the hot butter mixture could cause curdling but this sauce is not as prone to curdling as true Hollandaise sauce.

My Time Is _____ Min.

HOT POPPY SEED SAUCE

A touch of lemon softened by a hint of sweetness makes this a delightful sauce for any vegetable you wish to put it on. It is as easy as can be to make. You might also substitute sesame seed for the poppy seed for a change of pace.

Makes 1/2 cup   *Preparation time 2 Min.*

4 tablespoons butter or   1 teaspoon sugar
   margarine   Salt to taste
2 tablespoons lemon juice   Dash of liquid hot pepper
1 tablespoon poppy seed   sauce

Melt the butter in a measuring cup or small container. (This should take about 45 seconds.) Blend in the remaining ingredients. Heat in the microwave oven 30 to 60 seconds or until hot. Pour over the vegetable of your choice.

Tip: try this sauce on carrots to spark up the flavor. It also goes well on cabbage.

47

My Time Is _____ Min.

HOT ORANGE SAUCE

Try this with carrots, sweet potatoes, or any of the hard orange squashes. It adds a tang and interest that will have your eaters saying "Viva!"

Makes about 1 cup
- 2 tablespoons butter or margarine
- 2 tablespoons flour
- 2 tablespoons sugar
- 1/4 teaspoon ginger or cinnamon (see Tip)

Preparation time 7 Min.
- 1/4 teaspoon salt
- Dash of pepper
- 1 cup orange juice

Melt the butter in a 2-cup measure or small casserole in the microwave oven. (This will take about 45 to 60 seconds.) Stir in, until smooth, the flour, sugar, ginger or cinnamon, salt, and pepper. Blend in the orange juice. Cook in the microwave oven, stirring several times, until the sauce thickens and boils. (This will take about 3 to 3 1/2 minutes.) Continue cooking for 2 or 3 minutes more on defrost or low power. If these powers are not available, let the sauce sit for 2 minutes and then cook 1 minute more on **48** high.

Tip: use ginger if serving the sauce over carrots. If the sauce is for sweet potatoes or squash, use cinnamon. If you like a more mild orange taste, substitute water for some of the juice but use at least one-half juice.

My Time Is _____ Min.

THE ARTICHOKE

People either love or hate the way artichokes taste when cooked in the microwave oven the way most recipe books say they should be cooked. Go ahead and try them this way. You may be one of those who adore artichokes cooked in the microwave oven and just look at what you might have missed. After some experimentation I have found an alternate way of preparing artichokes that makes them taste much more like those cooked conventionally.

The artichoke is a member of the thistle family, yes, the common thistle you see growing along the roadside. The leaves and everything else are much larger than the weed variety. The part of the artichoke that is eaten is the flower bud and the leaf bracts that surround it. Artichokes can only be grown in places that have humid, cool climates. This is why they are so expensive. Artichokes were grown first in the lands that surround the central and western Mediterranean Sea and then spread east. At first the tender young leaves were eaten. The modern, edible-flowered artichoke was known in Italy around 1400 A.D. Supposedly Catherine de Medici took them with her when she went to France to marry the king. The French introduced the artichoke in the deep south while the Spanish introduced them into Califor- **49** nia. The plant is a perennial and is propagated by root divisions. The blooms can be dried and are used in many modern dried flower arrangements.

Look for artichokes that are bright green and that have plump leaves. If the leaves are plump and fresh looking but have a black "frosting," the artichoke has been frosted. This does not hurt the edibility of the plant. If the leaves look dry and are yellowing, then the vegetable is getting old and is past its prime. What are commonly called "baby" artichokes are lateral buds which are much smaller than the large, terminal buds. They are not younger or more tender than the large ones.

Selection

Look for plump, firm, tightly-closed buds. Buds that are opening, light in weight, or turning brown on the tips of the "petals" are past their prime. Frost can put a dark glaze on the outside of the artichoke but does not hurt its eating quality.

Preparation

First cut the stem off of the artichoke so that the "choke" will set flat and even. Next, with kitchen shears or a sharp knife, cut off the point of each leaf to remove the sharp, prickly tip. If the leaves at the base of the "choke" are tough and woody, remove them. Rinse and drain. Cook.

The way to eat an artichoke is as follows: pull a leaf off the vegetable. Hold the leaf by the upper end and dip the base of the leaf in the sauce, if one is used. Place the lower half of the leaf between your teeth. Use your teeth to scrape the soft material from the inside of the leaf. The remaining part of the leaf is discarded. Generally it is placed around the edge of the dish and each succeeding leaf is placed to overlap the preceeding leaf. As one gets nearer and nearer to the center of the choke the leaves get smaller until one reaches the "thistle" part. At this point remove and discard the thistle. With the tip of a spoon dig down into the "choke" bottom and remove the base of the thistle. If this is your first time to try artichokes, break one of the bottoms in half before removing the thistle base. You can then see a clear line that divides the edible and inedible portions. The base is considered the best part of the "choke" for it is all edible and one needn't work so hard to enjoy it.

50

Cooking

Fresh

The first way to try cooking an artichoke is to wrap each artichoke, individually, in wax paper or plastic wrap and cook it in its own steam. One medium-sized artichoke will cook in about 5 minutes. Test for doneness with a fork in the bottom of the choke. It should be just about tender. Allow for the residual cooking. Allow 11 to 12 minutes for 4 artichokes.

The second method most cookbooks advocate is to cook them in a covered casserole with about 1/4 cup water added. The method that gives a result most like conventional cooking is to put about 1 inch of water in a large casserole that will hold 4 large, 6 medium, or 8 small artichokes. Cook, covered, about 20 minutes or until the bottom of the choke is almost as tender as you wish it. The larger quantity of water and the longer cooking time give a more cooked flavor and make the vegetable more moist and mushy. Many people prefer this to the usual way of microwave cooking of artichokes. Either way, cook them to suit your own taste and enjoy them.

Frozen

Put the artichokes in a covered casserole icy-side up. Add 2 tablespoons water. Cook 3 minutes in the microwave oven on high. Separate and spread in a single layer. Cook 2 minutes more. Stir. Cook until tender. Let stand 5 minutes if they are to be eaten as is. If they are to be used in a dish such as Artichokes Au Gratin, eliminate the standing time.

Canned

These are precooked and can be used without any more precooking in any way desired.

Seasonings:	basil, coriander, curry powder, dill, garlic, horseradish, lemon, lime, nutmeg, onion, oregano, poppy seed, rosemary, sesame seed, tarragon, butter, salt, pepper
Sauces:	Bearnaise, Cream, Hollandaise, Mornay, and Tomato sauces; mayonnaise; sour cream
Cheeses:	Parmesan, Romano
Extra serving suggestions:	use melted butter or clarified butter use mayonnaise mixed with lemon juice and dill

51

ARTICHOKES WITH GARLIC BUTTER

One of the traditional ways of serving artichokes is to serve them with melted butter in which each "petal" base is dipped before being eaten. Here is a variation that makes for fine eating.

Makes 4 servings   *Preparation time 30 Min.*

4	artichokes (about 1 1/2 pounds)	1/2	cup butter	
1	cup water	1	clove garlic, minced	
		1	teaspoon lemon juice	

Wash the artichokes. Cut off the stem and the lower, tougher leaves. Cut off the top 3/4 inch of the artichokes. Set, stem-side down, in a large casserole. Add 1 cup water. Cook, covered, in the microwave oven for 12 minutes. Give each artichoke a half turn. Cover and continue cooking until the base tests tender when pricked with a fork, which should take about 8 to 12 minutes more. Drain and set aside.

Put 2 tablespoons of butter and the minced garlic in a small, covered dish in the microwave oven. Cook 2 minutes. Add the remaining butter and the lemon juice. Heat until the butter is melted and hot. Stir to blend.

52

Serve each artichoke with 1/4 of the butter mixture.

Tip: put the butter mixture in small, heated bowls so that it will stay warm.

My Time Is _____ Min.

GRATINÉE OF ARTICHOKE

Artichokes with a sauce that only the French could dream up. You will enjoy these time and time again. Not only that, but because these use the small artichokes, it is a more economical dish.

Makes 6 servings	Preparation time 40 Min.
6 small artichokes	2 tablespoons flour
1/2 cup water	1 teaspoon chicken bouillon
1 tablespoon lemon juice	concentrate
1 clove garlic, minced	1/4 teaspoon salt
(optional)	Dash of pepper
1/2 cup dried bread crumbs	1 1/2 cups milk or light cream
1 1/2 tablespoons butter	1/3 cup grated Swiss cheese
2 tablespoons butter, melted	

Remove the tough outer leaves from the artichoke. Cut off the stem-end, flush with the bottom of the choke. Put the artichokes, water, lemon juice, and garlic in a covered casserole. Cook about 15 minutes in the microwave oven or until a fork stuck in the bottom of the choke indicates the artichokes are tender. Let stand 10 minutes.

53

Meanwhile, put the bread crumbs and the 1 1/2 tablespoons of butter in a small dish and cook in the microwave oven until golden brown, stirring often to prevent overcooking and scorching in spots. (This should take only 2 to 3 minutes.) Set aside.

Cut the artichokes in half, lengthwise. Cut off the upper 1/3 of the leaf area. Place the artichokes in a circle around the outer edge of a casserole. Fill in the center area with the smaller pieces. Set aside. Melt the 2 tablespoons butter in a 1-quart casserole. Stir in the flour, bouillon concentrate, salt, and pepper. (The bouillon concentrate may need softening in a few spoonfuls of hot water.) Stir in the milk or light cream. Cook, covered, in the microwave oven for 4 1/2 minutes or until thick and bubbly, stirring several times during the last half of the cooking. Stir in the cheese. Let stand a minute, then stir to blend the cheese throughout the sauce. Pour the sauce over the artichoke halves. Sprinkle on the bread crumbs. Bake in the microwave oven until hot and bubbly (about 2 minutes).

(continued)

GRATINÉE OF ARTICHOKE (continued)

Tip: this dish is very rich, so it is best served with a simple roast or other such dish.

54

My Time Is _____ *Min.*

ARTICHOKES À LA GREECE

If this is your first try cooking artichokes, this is your recipe. If you have eaten artichokes all your life, this is your recipe too. These green globes need no other sauce or seasoning. Just enjoy!

Makes 4 servings

4 artichokes (about 1 1/2 pounds)
1 cup water
10 cardamom seeds (contents of about 3 pods)
2 cloves garlic

Preparation time 25 Min.

1 tablespoon lemon juice
1/4 teaspoon powdered thyme
1/4 teaspoon salt
Dash of white pepper
1/4 cup chopped parsley
1/3 cup olive oil.

Wash the artichokes. Cut off the stem and the lower, tougher leaves. Cut off the top 3/4 inch of the artichokes. Set, stem-side down, in a large casserole. Put the remaining ingredients in a blender and blend until smooth. Pour over the artichokes, spooning sauce over the cut off tops so that some of the sauce will run down inside the choke, flavoring it. Cook, covered, in the microwave oven for 10 minutes. Give each individual artichoke a half turn. Spoon more of the sauce over the tops. Cook, covered, until **55** tender, about 10 more minutes. Remove the artichokes to a dish and cover with plastic wrap or foil to keep warm and moist. Cook the sauce, uncovered, in the microwave oven until about 1/2 cup remains. Serve the artichokes with the remaining sauce spooned over them.

Tip: olive oil has a distinctive flavor. It is not recommended that another oil be used in its place. If olive oil is not available, then a substitute must be used but the flavor will not be quite the same.

My Time Is _____ *Min.*

ARTICHOKES NEWBURG

No, there is no shrimp or crab in Artichokes Newburg. It gets its name from the sauce which is very similar to that used in Shrimp Newburg. Many people are in doubt about how to properly eat artichokes. This recipe uses only the artichoke bottoms so the problem is eliminated.

Makes 6 servings *Preparation time 20 Min.*

- 1 package frozen artichoke bottoms (10 ounces)
- 1/4 cup chopped onion
- 1 cup water
- 3 tablespoons butter
- 3 tablespoons flour
- 1 1/2 cups light cream
- 1/8 teaspoon nutmeg
- Salt and pepper to taste
- 2 tablespoons Parmesan cheese
- 1 tablespoon chopped parsley

Put the artichoke bottoms, onion, and water in a covered casserole. Cook in the microwave oven until tender (about 10 to 12 minutes). Stir after 5 and 8 minutes of cooking respectively. Drain the remaining water into a small dish or casserole and set the artichokes aside.

56

Add the butter to the artichoke water. Put in the microwave and cook until the water has evaporated. The butter will be very bubbly at this stage. Stir in the flour. Blend in the cream. Add the nutmeg, salt, and pepper. Cook, covered, in the microwave oven until the mixture thickens and boils (about 4 to 5 minutes). It is very necessary to stir at least once each minute to prevent lumping and to keep the sauce smooth. Continue cooking for 2 or 3 minutes on defrost or low power. If these powers are not available, let the sauce sit for 2 minutes and then cook 1 minute more on high.

Pour the sauce over the artichoke bottoms, making certain each piece is coated with sauce. Sprinkle on the Parmesan cheese and the parsley. Return to the microwave oven and cook 1 minute more.

Tip: boiling off of the water mixed with the butter is to save the nutrients and the flavor without thinning the sauce. The butter holds the nutrients instead of letting them dry onto the cooking container.

My Time Is _____ Min.

ARTICHOKE OMELET

Most of the cooking time is used in making the omelets. They may be made on a browning tray in the microwave oven or on your conventional cooking unit. The filling is made in the microwave oven.

Makes 4 omelets
- 2 tablespoons butter or margarine
- 1/2 clove garlic, minced
- 1 cup chopped mushrooms
- 3 cooked artichoke hearts, diced
- Salt and pepper to taste

Preparation time 15 Min.
- Dash of cayenne
- 2 tablespoons tomato sauce
- 8 eggs
- 1 cup milk
- Butter to cook omelets, as needed

Put the butter, garlic, and mushrooms in a covered casserole and cook in the microwave oven for 4 minutes, stirring at least once. Add the artichoke hearts, salt, pepper, cayenne, and tomato sauce. Cook, covered, 4 minutes more, stirring at least once. While the filling is cooking, beat the eggs and milk until smooth. Make four omelets, cooking 1/4 of the batter at a time. As each omelet is done, place it on a plate. Put 1/4 of the filling along the middle of the omelet and fold first one side over the filling and then the other. Wipe any butter from the plate.

57

Tip: the omelet pan should be well buttered and be hot enough to make a drop of water dance before adding the eggs. After the edges set, raise them gently to let unset egg batter run under the edges to cook. When the egg begins to set well, shake from time to time to keep the egg from sticking to the pan.

My Time Is _____ Min.

ASPARAGUS

Asparagus is a member of the lily family and, in many forms, is native to much of Asia and Africa. This is a plant whose true leaves are reduced to scales. The edible varieties are grown throughout the temperate and sub-tropical areas of the world. It has been enjoyed by epicures since the days of the Roman Empire. The name comes from a Greek word meaning sprout and that is just the part that is eaten. The plant is herbaceous, that means the plant dies back to the ground each winter. In the spring, the tender, succulent sprouts that will become the stems and branchlets push up through the ground. This is the part that is eaten and is why fresh asparagus can be bought only in the springtime. The sprouts are harvested only over a 2 to 12 week period, depending on the age of the planting. If too many sprouts were harvested and some were not left to grow, the plant would be killed.

Asparagus is hand harvested. This is why it is so expensive. No mechanical method of harvest has been devised yet, as each sprout must be cut off just below the soil line. The woody base end of the sprout is left on to protect the succulent edible part of the asparagus from drying out too fast. When you are ready to **59** cook the asparagus, just snap off the woody end. The sprout, or spear as it is usually called, will break naturally just above the woody part.

About a third of the annual crop is sold fresh. The rest is either canned or frozen. Some asparagus is blanched so that it is white. This is done by mounding soil over the sprouts so that the sun does not reach them and so they will not start to produce chlorophyll which is what makes them green. The green sprouts are probably better for you nutritionally.

Selection

Look for asparagus that is firm, well formed, and has a tightly closed tip. If it has large or loose scales, these will often have to be pared away to remove the sand and dirt. Tough ends are left on the asparagus until cooking time to protect the freshness of the spears. Avoid stringy, limp asparagus and spears that are open and loose.

In microwave cooking it is especially important that you choose spears of the same thickness. Select fat or skinny stalks as you like but they should all be the same to allow even cooking.

Preparation

First snap off the tough base ends of the asparagus spears and discard them. Wash the asparagus well. If a lot of soil clings to them, use a vegetable brush on the stems, but not the tips, to remove the soil. If the scales on the lower stem are large or might hold dirt, peel them off. Now the plant is ready to cook.

Fresh or frozen asparagus is a difficult vegetable to cook whether it is cooked conventionally or by microwave. This is because it does not have the same density throughout. The tender, succulent tips cook before the heavier base part does.

Cooking

Fresh

If you wish to cook the asparagus cut up, you will have no difficulty with even cooking if you follow the instructions. After cleaning the vegetable, line the spears up with all the tender tips even. With a sharp knife (French chef's knife preferred) cut the asparagus into sections. Take the tougher, lower cuts and put them into a covered casserole with 1/4 cup water. Cook on high heat in the microwave oven several minutes or until the vegetable turns bright green. Then add the middle sections, stir, and cook, covered, for several minutes more or until the newly added sections are bright green. Add the tips, stir, and cook until almost tender enough. Remember to allow for the residual cooking.

60

If you wish to cook the asparagus in whole spears, use a rectangular baking dish. After preparing the spears (see above preparation section), place half the spears with the butt ends toward the end of the dish and the tips to the center. Place the remaining spears with the butt ends toward the other end of the dish and the spears to the center and preferably overlapping the tips of the other spears. This increases the functional density of the tender tips and slows down the cooking. Halfway through the cooking period mentally divide the cooking dish in fourths. Now turn each fourth over in such a manner that center spears are to the outside of the dish and the outside spears are in the center. Do not switch the stalks end for end. Cook until almost tender.

Frozen

If using frozen, cut asparagus, put it in a covered casserole and cook 8 to 9 minutes, stirring at least one time during the cooking period, for a 10-ounce package. The time varies according to the amount cooked. Again, allow for the residual cooking. Frozen produce takes less cooking than fresh as the freezing process breaks down some of the cellular material and overcooking makes it mushy.

Canned

This is a reheat process. Heat and use as you would fresh produce.

Seasonings:	chives, cloves, curry powder, dill, garlic, lemon, marjoram, mint, mustard, nutmeg, onion, parsley, poppy seed, sesame seed, butter, salt, pepper
Sauces:	Allemande, Bearnaise, Béchamel, Butter and Seed, Cheese, Garlic, Hollandaise, Hot Poppy Seed, Mornay, Parsley, Velouté, and White sauces; mayonnaise; sour cream
Cheeses:	American, Cheddar, Cream, Gruyère, Parmesan, Romano, Swiss
Wines:	chablis, rhine wine, sauterne
Nuts:	almonds, cashews, pine nuts
Extra serving suggestions:	hot, with cream, salt, and pepper
	hot, with slightly browned butter, Parmesan cheese, salt, and butter
	hot, with thick cream, cayenne, and salt
	hot, with lemon juice, salt, and pepper
	hot, with melted butter
	hot, with melted butter and lemon juice
	hot, with toasted buttered bread crumbs, chopped parsley, and chopped hard-boiled egg
	cold, with mayonnaise mixed with lemon juice
	cold, with olive oil, lemon juice, salt, and pepper
	cold, with olive oil, wine vinegar, salt, and pepper

ASPARAGUS WITH BUTTER AND PARMESAN CHEESE

Green produce comes from the microwave oven so green, so beautiful, and so nutritious, it should never be cooked any other way. Because it cooks so quickly, it retains more of its fresh-produce flavor.

Makes 4 servings
2 pounds fresh asparagus
1/4 cup water
1/4 cup melted butter

Preparation time 20 Min.
1/2 cup grated Parmesan cheese
Salt and pepper to taste

Snap off the tough ends of the asparagus and discard. Wash the asparagus thoroughly. If large stalks of asparagus are used, it may be wise to trim the lower scales off to aid in the removal of gritty dirt. Put the tips of the asparagus together evenly and, with a sharp knife, cut off any parts extending beyond about 6 inches. Cut these trimmings into 1-inch pieces. Place them in a covered casserole with the water. Cook in the microwave oven for 2 to 3 minutes, depending upon their toughness. Add the remaining asparagus, putting the butt ends toward the outer edges of the baking dish. Cover and cook until barely tender. (This should take about 6 to 8 minutes.)

62

Remove the asparagus to a serving dish, putting the cut pieces in the bottom of the dish and placing the spears attractively on top. Melt the butter in a small container in the microwave oven. Pour evenly over the asparagus. Sprinkle on the Parmesan cheese, salt, and pepper. Return to the microwave oven to reheat for 30 seconds.

Tip: the heavy, woody ends are left on asparagus to protect its moisture and quality during storage and shipping. Do not remove these until you are ready to use the vegetable. Try to choose spears of the same thickness for more even cooking.

My Time Is _____ Min.

ASPARAGUS
WITH GARLIC MAYONNAISE

Tasty and easy, what more can one ask of a recipe? Use with the first tender asparagus of spring. When that is no longer available, use it with the frozen asparagus spears from the freezer.

Makes 4 servings	Preparation time 15 Min.
2 pounds asparagus	1/2 teaspoon dill weed
1/4 cup water	1/4 teaspoon salt
1 cup mayonnaise	Dash of pepper
1/4 teaspoon powdered garlic	Pimiento strips (optional)
2 teaspoons lemon juice	

Snap off the tough ends of the asparagus. Wash thoroughly. If needed, pare or scrape off the larger scales. Place in a rectangular baking dish with half of the butt ends to one end of the dish and the other half to the other end. Add 1/4 cup water. Cover. Cook in the microwave oven until tender (about 10 to 12 minutes), rearranging once.

Mix the remaining ingredients thoroughly. Arrange the asparagus on a serving plate. Top with the sauce and garnish with the pimiento strips. If desired, put back in the microwave oven and cook about 1 minute longer to heat the sauce through.

63

Tip: the secret of even cooking of asparagus is to mentally divide the baking dish into quarters. Halfway through the cooking time, turn each quarter over still keeping the butt ends to the same end of the dish. In other words, the inside pieces become the outside pieces.

My Time Is _____ *Min.*

ASPARAGUS AND MUSHROOM SALAD

Here is a tossed salad utilizing some cooked and some raw produce. Use your microwave oven to cook the asparagus so as to retain its lovely color, nutrients, and flavor.

Makes 6 servings

- 4 tablespoons butter or oil
- 1/2 pound mushrooms, thickly sliced
- 1/2 pound asparagus tips, cut into 1-inch pieces
- 4 medium tomatoes, peeled and cut into wedges
- 1 green pepper, seeded and cut into strips

Preparation time 20 Min.

- 4 tiny sweet pickles, sliced
- 1 head Boston lettuce, torn into pieces
- 2 tablespoons wine vinegar
- 2 tablespoons salad oil
- 1 teaspoon salt
  Pepper to taste

Put the butter, mushrooms, and all but the tender tip pieces of the asparagus in a covered casserole and cook, covered, 5 minutes, stirring occasionally. Add the tips and cook, covered, 3 minutes more. Chill. Add all the other ingredients and toss well. Serve immediately.

64

Tip: if the tender asparagus tips were cooked as long as the rest of the spears, they would be mushy. Note the beautiful color contrast of the asparagus and the tomatoes.

My Time Is _____ Min.

ASPARAGUS WITH SOUR CREAM AND BACON

For a vegetable that is so delicious, this one takes very little time to prepare. It can be dressed up so that it is as pretty as it is tasty!

Makes 4 servings
- 2 pounds asparagus
- 1/4 cup water
- 1/2 cup sour cream
- 3 slices cooked bacon, crumbled

Preparation time 15 Min.
- 1 hard-boiled egg (cooked conventionally)
- Ripe olives (optional)

Wash the asparagus. Snap off the tough ends. If need be, scrape off the larger scales with a knife. Cook in a rectangular baking dish with half of the butt ends to one end of the dish and the other half to the other end of the dish and add the water. Cook, covered, in the microwave oven until the asparagus is bright green. Rearrange the spears so that those on the inside are put on the outside and those on the outside are pushed to the middle. Re-cover. Cook until the spears are barely tender.

65

Meanwhile, mix the sour cream and bacon. Peel and cut the egg into wedges. When the asparagus is done, put it in a serving dish. Pour on the sour cream mixture. Garnish with the egg wedges and olives.

Tip: try this sauce with green beans, broccoli, Brussels sprouts, and on and on and on. This is a good way to serve almost any green vegetable.

My Time Is _____ Min.

ASPARAGUS WITH SWISS CHEESE AND TOMATO SAUCE

Asparagus is one of the favorite vegetables of Italy. In the microwave oven, you will get a bonus in flavor and color that can be obtained in no other way. Try this classic dish.

Makes 4 servings
  2 pounds fresh asparagus
  1/4 cup water
  1/4 cup melted butter
  1 cup grated Swiss cheese

Preparation time 20 Min.
  1 can (8 ounces) tomato
      sauce
  Salt and pepper to taste

Snap off the tough ends of the asparagus and discard. Wash the asparagus thoroughly. If large stalks of asparagus are used, it may be wise to trim the lower scales off to aid in the removal of gritty dirt. Put the tips of the asparagus together evenly and, with a sharp knife, cut off any parts extending beyond 6 inches. Cut these trimmings into 1-inch pieces. Place them in a covered casserole with the water and butter. Cook in the microwave oven for 2 to 3 minutes, depending upon their toughness. Add the remaining asparagus, putting the butt ends toward the outer edges of the baking dish. Cover and cook just short of tenderness. (This should take about 6 minutes.)

66

In a 10″ × 6″ casserole, arrange the cut pieces of asparagus in a strip across the middle of the dish. Put half of the spears in a layer over this, keeping the butt ends against the edge of the dish and the tips across the strip of pieces. Sprinkle on 1/3 of the Swiss cheese. Put the other half of the asparagus in a second layer with the butt ends against the opposite side of the dish and the tips toward the center. Sprinkle on the second 1/3 of the Swiss cheese. Pour on the tomato sauce, covering the asparagus as evenly as possible. Sprinkle on the remaining cheese, then salt and pepper. Cook, covered, in the microwave oven 3 minutes more.

Tip: the heavy, woody ends are left on asparagus to protect its moisture and quality during shipping and storage. Do not remove these until you are ready to use the vegetable. Try to choose spears of approximately the same thickness for more even cooking.

My Time Is _____ Min.

THE AVOCADO

The avocado was one of the New World's contributions to good eating. This yellow green fleshed fruit, which contains no sugar, is usually used as a vegetable although there are recipes for avocado cake and avocado ice cream. It is mostly used in salads and only rarely cooked. Cooked, it is delicious, as in the recipes that follow or folded into an omelet or into scrambled eggs.

The avocado can range from the tiny seedless fruit that can be eaten in a few bites to some as large as a small cantaloupe. The skin may be black or dark green. The color "Avocado Green" is taken from the flesh of the fruit, not the skin. To check if an avocado is ripe, it should be slightly soft to the touch. Most avocados are picked before they are ripe so that they will ship better. Wrapping the fruit in a brown paper bag is supposed to hasten the ripening. When the avocado is ripe, it should be refrigerated until used.

Selection

Rarely are fully ripe avocados available in the market, so buy them from 3 to 5 days before they are to be used. Ripening is hastened by storing them in a warm, dark place. Once they are ripe, they can be held several more days by storing them in the refrigerator. Avocados are ripe when they are a little softer than a fully ripe pear. If they are mushy soft, they will have lost their good flavor. Under-ripe ones will have developed very little flavor.

Look for avocados with thick necks which often indicate greater quality. The thickness of the neck varies greatly with the variety. Summer ripening varieties often have very thick skin which makes testing for ripeness difficult.

Avoid fruit with black spots or bruises. Avocados should feel heavy for their size. A light feeling often indicates a fruit past its prime.

Preparation

Preparation of the avocado is very simple. Score the skin lightly with a knife as you would an orange and peel off the skin. Cut the avocado in half from the stem end downward and remove the single large seed. It is now ready to use.

As avocados turn dark and brown easily due to exposure to the air, do not prepare until ready to use. If preparation is needed in advance, brush all surfaces with lemon juice and wrap in plastic wrap until it is time to use it. Rinse off the juice before using, and blot dry, as the lemon juice may affect the flavor of a dish in which the taste of lemon is not desired.

Cooking

Fresh

Be careful of overcooking the avocado. Since this product is high in both water and oil content, usually cooking long enough to heat thoroughly is all that is needed.

Frozen

Avocados are not available frozen except as dip mixtures.

Canned

Avocados are not available canned.

68 *Seasonings:*	cayenne, garlic, lemon, onion, salt, pepper
Sauce:	Garlic
Cheeses:	Parmesan, Romano
Wine:	dry vermouth
Extra serving suggestions:	best served as Guacamole (See recipe for Mushrooms stuffed with Guacamole)
	use in omelets
	use in salads
	use in sandwiches
	stuff with chicken, tuna, etc.

AVOCADO-TOMATO BAKE

Try this tasty, beautiful casserole any time of the year. Although more expensive in the winter, it is a good way to break the winter eating blahs. It is a joy to serve any time at all.

Makes 6 servings

2 tablespoons butter	1 pound tomatoes, peeled and cut into eighths
1 small clove garlic, minced	
1/4 cup dry bread crumbs	1/4 cup grated Parmesan cheese
1 tablespoon butter	
1/4 pound mushrooms, sliced	1 ripe avocado
1 medium onion cut into wedges	

Preparation time 15 Min.

Put the 2 tablespoons butter and garlic in a small dish or casserole. Cook, covered, in the microwave oven for 1 minute. Add the bread crumbs and return to the microwave oven. Cook, uncovered, stirring often, until the crumbs are toasted, which will take about 3 minutes. Set aside.

Put the 1 tablespoon butter, mushrooms, and onion in a larger, covered casserole. Cook in the microwave oven, stirring once after 3 minutes, until tender (about 6 minutes). Add the tomatoes and continue cooking 2 minutes more. Remove from the oven. **69**

Stir the grated Parmesan cheese into the bread crumbs. Sprinkle the crumb mixture evenly over the vegetables.

Peel the avocado. Cut in half from top to bottom. Gently pull the halves apart and remove the seed. Cut each half into 4 strips. Place the 8 strips on top of the casserole spoke fashion with the bigger end to the outer edge of the dish. Cook, uncovered, 2 1/2 minutes to heat the avocado through.

Tip: to peel the tomatoes easily, drop for a few moments into boiling water. Remove with a slotted spoon and drop into cool water. The skin will almost slip off. Do not peel the avocado ahead of time as it turns dark (oxidizes) just like an apple when exposed to the air.

My Time Is _____ Min.

BAKED AVOCADO SUPREME

Avocados are so delicious raw that many people never think about cooking them. This recipe is both different and delicious. Try it as an accompaniment to meat or fish.

Makes 4 servings
- 2 ripe avocados
- 2 teaspoons lime or lemon juice
- 1/2 teaspoon powdered onion
- 1/8 teaspoon powdered garlic (or to taste)
- 1/8 teaspoon chili powder (or to taste)

Preparation time 4 Min.
- Salt and pepper to taste
- 6 tablespoons finely-minced tomato
- 3 tablespoons finely-minced onion

Cut the avocados in half and remove the seed. Carefully scoop out all the pulp leaving the shells intact. Mash the pulp until it is smooth. Blend in the lime or lemon juice, powdered onion, powdered garlic, chili powder, salt, and pepper. Spoon the pulp back into the shells. Make an indentation in the middle of the filling of each of the shells. Mix the tomato and onion, then divide evenly and spoon into the depression in the filling. Cook, uncovered, in the microwave oven until quite hot throughout. (This should take from 1 to 1 1/2 minutes.)

70

Tip: to tell when these are done, feel the outside of the shells. When they are piping hot, the cooking is finished.

My Time Is _____ Min.

AVOCADO, CHEESE, AND BACON BAKE

An avocado combination that is so delicious, rich, and satisfying it could be a luncheon entrée instead of a vegetable. Either way, you will want to enjoy it time and time again.

Makes 4 servings   *Preparation time 15 Min.*

4 slices bacon	1/2 cup milk
2 ripe avocados	Salt to taste
1/3 cup finely-diced onion	Chili powder to taste
1 tablespoon butter	3/4 cup shredded cheese,
1 tablespoon flour	Cheddar or American

Cook the bacon on paper toweling in the microwave oven until crisp (about 4 minutes or 1 minute per slice). Meanwhile, peel the avocado, remove the pit, and dice the avocado. Put the onion and the butter in a 2-cup measure or a small casserole. Cook it for 3 minutes in the microwave oven. Stir in the flour and then slowly blend in the milk. Cook, stirring several times, in the oven until the sauce thickens (about 2 minutes). Continue cooking for 2 or 3 minutes more on defrost or low power. If these powers are not available, let the sauce sit for 2 minutes and then cook 1 minute more on high. Stir in the salt, chili powder, and 1/2 cup of the shredded cheese and blend well. Crumble and stir in the bacon. Gently fold in the avocado cubes. Place in a shallow baking dish. Sprinkle with the remaining 1/4 cup shredded cheese. Cook 1 minute in the microwave oven or until the mixture is hot and the cheese has melted.

Tip: the best way to cook bacon in the microwave oven is to place one paper towel for each slice of bacon on a paper plate. Then add the bacon and top with one more sheet of paper toweling. Cook about 1 minute for each slice of regular thickness bacon. Extra thick bacon needs longer cooking.

My Time Is _____ Min.

BEANS

Broad beans, like the fava and horsebeans, were grown in Europe since prehistoric times. The "green bean," as well as many other types, were not known in Europe until after the discovery of the Americas. Although a product of Central and South America, the "green bean" became known in many countries as the "french bean," the haricot of French cooking.

In general, varieties grown as "dry beans" have a pod too coarse for eating. Those grown for their edible pods have seeds too small or too few to bother with for "dry beans."

Beans are many shades of green, yellow, off white, red, brown, and purple and range in size from the large beans like the lima and butter beans to the mung bean which is used mainly to produce bean sprouts. The bean family is very diverse and has a very important place in the world's food supply.

GREEN BEANS

Selection

In green beans look for firm but tender pods without brown spots. Select all the pods as nearly the same size and diameter as is possible to allow even cooking. Beans picked too young have very poor keeping quality and should be used at once. Beans picked too mature will be tough and tasteless.

Preparation

Remove the ends of the beans and any strings they may have. The strings, if any, are found along the inside curve. Wash and drain. The beans can be cooked whole, cut into lengthwise strips (French or julienne), or cut crosswise into pieces. They can also be cut on the diagonal.

Like most vegetables, the age or maturity of the produce has a great deal of effect on the cooking time. When buying fresh green beans, try to select, as far as is possible, beans of the same size to facilitate even cooking. There is no way to cook skinny and fat beans together without overcooking the skinny ones or undercooking the fat ones.

Green beans need more standing time to allow for residual cooking than most vegetables. It is amazing how much more done they taste after 5 to 10 minutes standing time. If the beans should cool down a little, a minute or two in the microwave oven will bring them back to serving temperature.

Cooking

Fresh

If the beans are to be cooked whole, for 1 pound of beans use 1/2 cup water. The cooking container should be a large, preferably oval or rectangular, covered casserole. A loaf pan covered with plastic wrap or wax paper is good. Place the beans parallel in the cooking container, cover, and cook 4 minutes in the microwave oven. Turn the beans so those on the inside of the food mass are on the outside and those on the outside are on the inside. Cover. Cook 4 minutes more. Rearrange the beans as described above. Cover. Cook 4 minutes more or as needed to make beans tender. As you rearrange the beans make sure that any beans that do not look done enough (they will be a lighter green) are pushed to the outside. Usually 12 to 15 minutes will be enough cooking time. Allow 5 to 10 minutes standing time. If the beans cool too much they may be reheated in the microwave oven with no loss of quality.

74

For cut beans, cut the beans into the desired length. The smaller each piece is cut, the quicker the beans will cook as more surface area is created to absorb microwaves. Use 1/2 cup water to 1 pound of beans. Cook, covered, in the microwave oven, stirring several times to obtain even cooking, until the beans are tender. (This should take from 10 to 14 minutes.) Allow 5 to 10 minutes standing time for residual cooking. If the beans cool too much they may be reheated in the microwave oven with no loss of quality.

For French-style or julienne beans, cut the prepared beans lengthwise several times with a knife or put through a bean slicer. Use 1/2 cup water to 1 pound of beans. Cook, covered, in the microwave oven, stirring several times to obtain even cooking, until the beans are tender. This should take about 10 to 14 minutes. Allow 5 to 10 minutes standing time for residual cooking. If the beans cool too much they may be reheated in the microwave oven with no loss of quality.

Frozen

For whole green beans, put the package of beans (10 ounces) and 1/4 cup water in a covered casserole and cook in the microwave oven until tender. (This will take about 8 to 10 minutes.) It is best to use a rectangular or oval container and to lay the beans parallel. The beans must be rearranged twice during the cooking period for even cooking. Beans on the inside must be moved to the outside on the first rearrangement. During the second rearrangement, any beans that are of a lighter hue should be moved to the outside of the dish. Allow 5 minutes standing time.

For cut beans, regular- or Italian-style, put the package of beans (10 ounces) and 2 tablespoons water in a covered casserole and cook in the microwave oven until tender. (This will take about 8 minutes.) Stirring is necessary and seems best when done after 4 and 6 minutes of cooking respectively. Use your timer to remind you to stir by setting it for 4 minutes, then 2 minutes, and then 2 minutes more or as long as is needed to finish cooking the beans. Allow 5 minutes standing time.

For frozen julienne (French-style) beans put the package of beans (9 ounces) in a covered casserole. Because the beans have been sliced and therefore have more surfaces to exude liquid, it is rare that any extra liquid is needed. If the beans seem extra dry, 1 tablespoon of water may be added. Cook, covered, in the microwave until tender (about 8 minutes). Stir at the end of 4 and 6 minutes respectively. Let stand 5 minutes.

75

Canned

Canned beans are fully cooked and need only reheating.

Seasonings:	basil, caraway, chives, dill, fennel, garlic, lemon, mint, mustard, nutmeg, onion, oregano, paprika, parsley, poppy seed, savory, sesame seed, tarragon, thyme, butter, salt, pepper
Sauces:	Allemande, Bearnaise, Béchamel, Butter and Seed, Mornay, and Tomato sauces; sour cream; yogurt; French dressing
Cheeses:	American, Blue, Cheddar, Cream, Gruyère, Parmesan, Romano, Swiss
Wines:	chablis, rhine wine, sauterne, sherry, vermouth
Nuts:	almonds, cashews, peanuts, pine nuts, water chestnuts

suggestions: hot, with crumbled bacon, cooked onion, and mushrooms

cooked with diced ham

hot, with garlic powder, butter, salt, and pepper

cooked with diced red pepper and chopped onion for color and flavor contrast

LIMA BEANS

Selection

In lima beans, or other such fresh beans, try to pick young pods so that the beans will be young and tender. Fat, mature beans will be starchy and will need to be cooked covered with water. Lima beans are always eaten shelled. Try to select pods having the same thickness and maturity to allow even cooking.

Preparation

76 Open the outer bean pod and remove the seeds. The pods are not edible and are discarded. The beans may be rinsed and then are ready for use. Allow about 3 ounces per serving.

Cooking

Fresh

The maturity, the water content, and the amount of starch in the beans will greatly affect the cooking time and the amount of water needed in the cooking. If the beans are produced commercially, the chances are high that they will be quite mature. In that case these beans must be treated almost like a dry bean in that much water will be used and a relatively long cooking time will be needed. One pound of beans will take up to 2 cups water and will cook about 20 to 30 minutes.

If you grow your own beans, pick them when they are young and tender. The quality and the flavor will be greatly superior. For 1 pound of beans 1 cup of water will probably suffice and a cooking time of 15 to 20 minutes will be enough.

Frozen

Because of the high starch and low water content of frozen lima and baby lima beans, there is no appreciable difference in cooking times and techniques from those for fresh beans. A 10-ounce package of commercially frozen beans will take 1 cup of water and about 15 minutes cooking time. Butter Beans take about 8 minutes.

Again, if home grown, home frozen beans are used, and if they were picked when less mature, the cooking times will be shortened.

Canned

Canned beans are precooked and need only be reheated.

Dried

See dried beans.

Seasonings:	basil, chives, garlic, lemon, onion, oregano, parsley, savory, thyme, butter, salt, pepper
Sauces:	Béchamel, Butter and Seed, Mornay, Tomato and White sauces; sour cream
Cheeses:	American, Cheddar, Cream, Gruyère, Parmesan, Swiss
Wine:	chablis
Nuts:	pine nuts, sunflower seed, water chestnuts
Extra serving suggestions:	hot, with crumbled bacon, cooked onion hot, cooked with diced ham hot, with pimiento and onions

BEAN SPROUTS

Selection

Bean sprouts should be creamy white, crisp, and free of any browning when selected. Try to use them within 24 hours of purchase.

Preparation

Rinsing and draining are the only preparation needed as this vegetable product is eaten as is. Bean sprouts do not keep well so plan to use them as soon as possible after purchasing. Do not buy those that are turning brown as they are already past their prime. The bean sprouts most often used are those of the mung bean.

Cooking

Fresh

Cook in a covered casserole, stirring a time or two, just until the sprouts have lost their stiffness. Be very careful of overcooking as they lose all texture very easily. Half of the pleasure of eating bean sprouts is their slight crunchiness. Once the stiffness is gone, the residual cooking will usually be enough to make them tender without overcooking.

If the bean sprouts are to be used with other foods, be even more careful of overcooking as the heat from the other foods will also add to the residual cooking effect.

78

Frozen

Not usually available frozen. They are usually included in with other foods when frozen and need only be heated through thoroughly for the sprouts to be done.

Canned

Canned products are fully cooked and need only be reheated.

Seasonings:	chili powder, curry powder, garlic, lemon, onion, parsley, sesame seed, butter, salt, pepper, sugar, soy sauce
Sauces:	Béchamel, Butter and Seed, Cheese, Garlic, Mornay, Tomato Sauce Provençal, Velouté, White
Cheeses:	Monterey Jack, Parmesan
Wines:	chablis, rhine wine, sauterne, sherry, vermouth
Nuts:	cashews, peanuts, sunflower seed

Extra serving
suggestions: cook with onion and parsley

cook with edible pod peas, season with soy sauce

cook with mushrooms, a dab of chicken bouillon, and thicken with corn starch

cook with water chestnuts, green onions, and soy sauce

DRIED BEANS

Selection

Usually beans are prepackaged so there is no selection other than selecting the type that will give the flavor and color desired.

Preparation

Sort through the beans and remove any obviously damaged ones. Remove any foreign matter. Be especially alert for small pieces of rock. Where does it come from? That isn't important but from time-to-time small stones are found in beans. Wash and drain the beans. Presoaking for 8 to 12 hours will cut about 10 minutes off the cooking time.

Cooking

Dried

Use as large a microwave oven-proof container as you have. Put in the beans, 1 tablespoon butter, margarine, or oil, and enough water to cover the beans by at least 1 inch. Cook 10 minutes, stir, and add enough water to bring it back to 1 inch above the beans. Repeat this procedure 3 times at 10-minute intervals. Then repeat at 15-minute intervals until the beans are done. Altogether, the beans will soak up about 4 times their measure in water.

It takes about 1 hour and 40 minutes to cook 1/2 pound beans. One pound of beans cooks in about 2 hours. The time will vary with the type and amount of beans being cooked. It is best to cook beans well in advance of their planned use and to then reheat them. This eliminates the last minute rush trying to get them done in time.

Beans tend to boil over easily. The butter helps prevent this to some degree. If your oven has a simmer or slow speed, use it during the last half of the cooking period. It is a wise idea to set the cooking container in a larger dish. Then if the beans boil over, the liquid is contained in the outer dish. At any rate, the microwave oven is certainly easier to clean than your stove top burner if it does boil over.

Seasonings:	chili powder, coriander, cumin (comino), curry powder, garlic, lemon, marjoram, mint, mustard, nutmeg, onion, paprika, parsley, poppy seed, sage, savory, sesame seed, butter, salt, pepper, sugar, brown sugar, honey, molasses
Sauce:	Tomato
Cheeses:	American, Cheddar, Monterey Jack, Mozzarella, Provolone
Wines:	burgundy, claret, sauterne, sherry
Extra serving suggestions:	this is too wide a field for individual serving suggestions

GREEN BEANS ALMONDINE

Why serve plain beans when they can be made outstanding with such little effort? Try this classic recipe in the microwave oven.

Makes 4 servings

1	clove garlic, minced
1	tablespoon butter or margarine
1	pound green beans
1/2	cup water

Preparation time 20 Min.

1	tablespoon butter or margarine
1/4	cup sliced almonds
	Salt and pepper to taste

Put the garlic and 1 tablespoon butter in a covered casserole in the microwave oven and cook 2 minutes.

Prepare the beans by snipping off the ends and removing any strings. Wash, drain, and cut into bite-sized pieces. Add the beans and water to the butter and garlic and cook, covered, in the microwave oven, stirring several times, until the beans are tender. (This should take from 10 to 15 minutes.) Drain the liquid into a small casserole or dish. Set the beans aside.

Add the remaining 1 tablespoon butter to the liquid and cook, uncovered, until the liquid is reduced and the butter is hot and bubbly. Add the nuts, stir, and continue cooking, stirring frequently, until the nuts are toasted. (This should take about 2 or 3 minutes.) **81**

Add the toasted nuts and butter to the beans. Add the salt and pepper and stir well to coat the beans.

Tip: the nuts need frequent stirring so they will brown evenly. Slivered almonds may also be used in place of the sliced almonds.

My Time Is _____ Min.

GREEN BEANS AND ONIONS

The following recipe has a basic recipe and an alternate one. Both are excellent and should be used often. Good, simple food, easily prepared, is a joy.

Makes 4 servings

- 1/2 pound green beans or
    - 1 10-ounce package frozen green beans
- 1/4 cup water
- 1/2 pound tiny boiling onions
- 1 tablespoon butter

Preparation time 25 Min.

- 2 strips crisply-cooked bacon
- Salt and pepper to taste
- 1 cup sauce (Béchamel, Parsley, or White) optional

Break the stem-end off of the beans and remove any strings along the curved side. Cut the beans into 1-inch lengths. Put the beans and the water in a covered casserole. Cook in the microwave oven, stirring twice, until tender. Fresh beans take about 10 to 12 minutes to cook. The frozen beans will take about 8 minutes. Set the beans aside.

82 While the beans are cooking, peel the onions. Put the onions and the butter in a covered casserole. Cook in the microwave oven, stirring once, until tender (about 5 to 6 minutes). Add to the beans.

Drain the liquid from the vegetables. If they are to be eaten without the sauce, reduce the liquid by boiling in a small dish or casserole in the microwave oven until only the butter remains. Add the butter to the vegetables. Crumble the bacon and add it and the salt and pepper. Stir gently to mix. Reheat a minute or two in the microwave oven, if it is needed.

If the sauce is to be used, use the drained liquid as part of the liquid in the sauce. Crumble the bacon and add it and the sauce to the vegetables. If need be, reheat a minute or two in the microwave oven.

Tip: always cook the green beans first. No other vegetable needs standing time to develop its flavor as do green beans.

My Time Is _____ Min.

GREEN BEANS WITH PEPPERS SALAD

Most Scandinavian salads are cooked salads, as the Scandinavian growing season for salad greens is very short. It is costly to import greens, so do not look for many recipes for tossed salads in Scandinavian cookery.

Makes 4 servings   *Preparation time 25 Min.*
- 1   pound green beans   Pepper to taste
- 1/4 cup water   1   large green pepper
- 1/2 cup salad oil   2   tablespoons crumbled
- 2   tablespoons wine vinegar   blue cheese
- 2   teaspoons minced parsley 1/2 cup sour cream
- 1/2 teaspoon salt   1/2 teaspoon dill weed

Snip off and discard the ends from the green beans and remove any strings. Cut the beans lengthwise. Put the beans and water in a covered casserole and cook for 10 to 12 minutes in the microwave oven, until tender. Drain. Mix the salad oil, vinegar, parsley, salt, and pepper. Pour over the beans and mix well. Cover and refrigerate, stirring from time-to-time.

When ready to serve, drain the beans and save the marinade. **83** Seed the green pepper and cut into thin strips. Add to the beans. Blend the blue cheese, sour cream, and enough of the marinade to thin to the desired dressing consistency. Stir in the dill weed. Pour over the salad before serving.

Tip: cook the beans until they are just barely tender, as there will be enough residual cooking to finish tenderizing them. For a nice color contrast, stir in 2 tablespoons diced pimiento.

My Time Is _____ Min.

GREEN BEANS SUPREME

There must be other recipes given the same name but you will find this one delightfully satisfying. While the recipe calls for fresh beans, canned or frozen beans may be substituted. Canned mushrooms may also be substituted. Fresh produce is so good that, when possible, it is recommended.

Makes 6 servings

- 1 pound green beans, cut into 1/2-inch lengths
- 1/2 pound mushrooms, sliced
- 1/4 cup water
- 2 tablespoons butter or margarine
- 2 tablespoons flour

Preparation time 23 Min.

- 1 teaspoon chicken bouillon concentrate
- 1 cup liquid, reserved liquid plus milk
- Salt and pepper to taste
- 1 cup crisp french fried onions

Put the green beans, mushrooms, and water in a 1 1/2-quart covered casserole and cook, stirring several times, in the microwave oven until the beans are almost tender. Drain and reserve any liquid from the beans. Set the beans aside.

84 Melt the butter in the microwave oven in a small casserole. Stir in the flour and the chicken bouillon concentrate. Blend in the 1 cup liquid, salt, and pepper. Cook, stirring several times, in the microwave oven until the sauce comes to a boil. Continue cooking for 2 or 3 minutes more on defrost or low power. If these powers are not available, let the sauce sit for 2 minutes and then cook 1 minute more on high.

Gently stir the sauce into the beans. Top with the french fried onions. Cook, uncovered, in the microwave oven just long enough to reheat. If the casserole is being made ahead of time, do not add the french fried onions until the beans are heated through or they will not stay crisp.

Tip: if using canned beans and/or mushrooms, drain the liquid and reduce to about 1/2 cup or less. Use this reduced liquid in cooking or heating the beans and mushrooms. It will also become part of the sauce.

My Time Is _____ Min.

GREEN BEANS AND RED POTATOES

Due to the difficulty of getting the beans and the potatoes done at the same time, it is suggested that each vegetable be cooked separately before combining them. The flavor is superb. This is a good recipe for cooking ahead and then reheating.

Makes 6 servings   *Preparation time 33 Min.*

1 pound green beans	1 cup liquid (liquid from
1 teaspoon chicken bouillon	vegetables plus milk)
concentrate	2 tablespoons butter or
1/2 cup water	margarine
1 pound red potatoes	2 tablespoons flour
(approximately)	Salt and pepper to taste

Always cook the green beans first. They benefit from the extra standing time. Snip the ends and any strings from the green beans. Wash and drain. Cut into 1/2-inch pieces. Put the green beans, chicken bouillon concentrate, and the 1/2 cup water in a covered casserole and cook, stirring several times, in the microwave oven until tender. (This should take 10 to 15 minutes.)

Peel, wash, drain, and dice the potatoes into 1/2-inch pieces. Put **85** into a covered casserole. When the beans are done, drain the liquid into the potatoes. Cook the potatoes, covered, in the microwave oven, stirring several times, until tender (about 10 to 12 minutes). Drain the liquid into a 1-cup measure and finish filling with milk.

Melt the butter in a small container in the microwave oven. Stir in the flour. Blend in the liquid. Cook until thickened in the microwave oven, stirring several times. Continue cooking for 2 or 3 minutes more on defrost or low power. If these powers are not available, let the sauce sit for 2 minutes and then cook 1 minute more on high. Combine the beans, potatoes, and sauce. Season with salt and pepper. Reheat until piping hot.

Tip: if you like a richer sauce, use light cream (half and half) or heavy cream (whipping cream). New potatoes are equally good in place of the red potatoes.

My Time Is _____ *Min.*

SWEET AND SOUR GREEN BEANS

Wow! What a way to liven-up green beans! The flavor sparkles and sings. Try it with fresh, frozen, or even canned beans.

Makes 6 servings   Preparation time 35 Min.

4	slices bacon	1	tablespoon soy sauce
1	pound fresh green beans	1/4	cup chopped sweet pickle
1/2	cup water	1 1/2	cups liquid (liquid from
3	tablespoons sugar		beans plus water)
3	tablespoons vinegar	1	green pepper, sliced
3	tablespoons cornstarch		

Cook the bacon on paper toweling in the microwave oven until brown and crisp (about 4 minutes). Set aside. Snap off the ends of the beans and cut into 1 1/2-inch pieces. Put in a casserole with the water and cook, covered, in the microwave oven, stirring several times, until the beans are tender (about 10 to 15 minutes). Drain and reserve the bean liquor. Set the beans aside.

In another covered casserole, mix the sugar, vinegar, cornstarch, soy sauce, and sweet pickle. Add enough water to the bean liquor to bring the liquid up to 1 1/2 cups. Stir into the sauce mixture. Stir in the green pepper. Cook, covered, in the microwave oven, stirring several times, until the mixture comes to a boil (about 6 minutes). When the sauce has thickened and come to a boil, continue cooking for 2 to 3 minutes more on defrost or low power. If these powers are not available, let the sauce sit for 2 minutes and then cook 1 minute more on high. Add the beans and crumbled bacon. Cook, covered, until heated through.

Tip: use 2 packages frozen green beans and cook, with 1/4 cup added liquid, in the microwave oven until they are tender (about 10 to 12 minutes.) Use the liquid that results as part of the liquid needed for the sauce. If using canned beans, they need only be heated, so no precooking is necessary. Just drain and use the liquor as part of the sauce liquid. After the sauce is cooked, add the beans and heat.

My Time Is _____ Min.

BABY LIMAS AND BACON

Here is a traditional way to cook lima beans. The difference here is that you are making use of modern technology. Use the packages of frozen beans from the freezer and your microwave oven. Old-fashioned goodness with modern convenience.

Makes 4 servings   *Preparation time 20 Min.*

  3 slices bacon, diced   1 package (10 ounces)
  1 cup hot tap water   frozen baby lima beans
1/4 teaspoon salt

Cook the bacon in a large casserole, stirring once, until lightly browned (about 3 minutes). Discard all but 2 to 4 tablespoons of the bacon fat. Add the hot water slowly and then the remaining ingredients. The addition of hot water is to prevent the cracking of the casserole. Cover and cook in the microwave oven, stirring several times, until the beans are tender (about 12 to 15 minutes). Let stand 5 minutes before serving.

Tip: if using fresh beans from your garden, it is probable that they will be younger, more tender, and contain less starch. For these reasons, the cooking time may be less. **87**

My Time Is _____ *Min.*

CRUNCHY BEAN SPROUTS

Here is a really nice, refreshing, light vegetable to be served with Polynesian or oriental foods. So quick and easy, you will be delighted.

Makes 4 servings		*Preparation time 10 Min.*	
3	slices bacon	1	tablespoon soy sauce
10	ounces fresh bean sprouts	1/4	teaspoon ground ginger
1	green onion, thinly sliced	1/2	teaspoon monosodium
1	teaspoon cornstarch		glutamate (MSG)

Cook the bacon on paper toweling in the microwave oven until crisp (about 3 minutes). Set aside. Put all the other ingredients in a covered casserole and stir. Cook, covered, in the microwave oven stirring once or twice until just barely tender. Crumble the bacon and sprinkle on top. Serve with additional soy sauce.

Tip: do not overcook! There will be a fair amount of residual cooking taking place by the time the food is on the table and everyone is served. The bean sprouts should be tender-crisp, not limp.

88

My Time Is _____ Min.

BEAN SPROUTS AND GREEN PEPPERS

Two vegetables that complement each other beautifully are combined in this recipe. True to Oriental-style cooking, the texture should be tender-crisp. Also allow for the residual cooking when judging the doneness of each vegetable.

Makes 4 servings   *Preparation time 10 Min.*

- 1/4 cup chopped onion
- 1 tablespoon butter or margarine
- 2 medium-sized green peppers
- 1 teaspoon soy sauce (or to taste)

- 1 teaspoon cornstarch
- 1 tablespoon water
- 1/2 pound bean sprouts
   Salt and pepper to taste

Put the onion and butter in a covered casserole. Cook in the microwave oven for 3 minutes. Meanwhile, core and slice the green peppers. Add the peppers to the onions. Mix the soy sauce, cornstarch, and water. Stir into the vegetables. Continue cooking, stirring several times, until the peppers are barely tender (about 5 minutes). Stir in the bean sprouts. Continue cooking for 1 minute. Stir. Continue cooking until the bean sprouts start to lose **89** their crispness. Add the salt and pepper. Serve.

Tip: allow for the residual cooking. In general, there is about a 5-minute lag from when the last food is cooked and when the family has seated itself, been served, and actually starts to eat. Tender vegetables can overcook very easily.

My Time Is _____ *Min.*

RICE AND BEAN SPROUTS

Here a succulent vegetable and a starchy one are combined in one tasty, appetizing dish. The chopped onion gives a pretty emerald touch.

Makes 4 servings	*Preparation time 10 Min.*
3 tablespoons sesame seed	1 clove garlic, minced
1 teaspoon oil or butter	1 1/2 cups fresh bean sprouts
1/4 cup chopped green onion tops	2 tablespoons soy sauce
	2 cups hot, cooked rice

Combine the sesame seed and the oil in a small dish and cook in the microwave oven, stirring often, until the seeds are lightly toasted (about 2 minutes). Set aside. In a covered casserole, combine the onion, garlic, and bean sprouts and cook, covered, stirring several times, until the bean sprouts are just beginning to get tender. (This will take only 2 or 3 minutes.) Stir in the sesame seed and soy sauce. Gently mix in the rice. Be careful not to mash the ingredients.

90 **Tip:** if the rice has cooled, reheat it in the microwave oven. It reheats beautifully. Do this before mixing so as not to overcook the vegetables. The bean sprouts should be cooked until they just begin to lose their stiffness, as their own heat and the heat of the rice will finish the job.

My Time Is _____ Min.

GREEK-STYLE BAKED BEANS

Try these baked beans that are quite different from the usual run-of-the-mill baked beans. Rosemary is the main seasoning agent and makes a very tasty flavor combination.

Makes 6 servings   *Preparation time 2 hours*

1/2 pound small white beans	1/4 cup dry red wine
1 1/2 cups water, add more as needed	1/2 teaspoon dry basil
	1/2 teaspoon finely-chopped rosemary (1 teaspoon, if fresh)
1 tablespoon butter	
1/2 teaspoon salt	
1/2 cup chopped onion	1/4 teaspoon dry mustard
1 clove garlic, minced	1/2 teaspoon salt
1/4 cup olive or salad oil	Pepper to taste
3 tablespoons tomato paste	1/4 cup grated Romano or Parmesan cheese
1 bay leaf broken in two	
1/4 cup honey	

Put the beans, water, butter, and 1/2 teaspoon salt in a large, covered casserole and cook in the microwave oven until tender. (This will take about 1 hour and 40 minutes.) Add water and stir, at first every 10 minutes and then every 15 minutes, while the beans are cooking. Set the beans aside.

91

Put the onion, garlic, and oil in a small casserole and cook, covered, 4 minutes in the microwave oven. Stir in the tomato paste, bay leaf, honey, wine, basil, rosemary, mustard, salt, and pepper. Add to the beans and mix well. Put the beans in an 8″ × 8″ casserole and cook, uncovered, in the microwave oven 10 minutes more, stirring at least 2 times. Sprinkle on the cheese. Let stand 5 minutes before serving.

Tip: if the beans are soaked overnight, or all day, before cooking, the cooking time is reduced to 1 hour and 25 minutes. Use the olive oil if possible as it adds a special flavor.

My Time Is _____ Min.

BEETS

The beet, or beetroot, is a biennial. During its first year the beet forms the thick taproot that is eaten. During the second year it blooms and sets its seeds.

It is a very important plant. There are three main types of beets used for food. The most important form is the *sugar beet* from which we obtain much of our sugar and, also, much animal feed. The second type is the *garden beet* which provides those dark red globes we eat and also gives us beet greens, one of the tastier forms of greens. The third form is the *leaf beet* which is much better known as *Chard*. Chard is also used as a green. One advantage of chard is that it tolerates more warm weather than most greens and therefore lengthens the season in which greens are available.

Selection

Choose beets that are young and tender for the best flavor. At this stage, the tops can be used as "greens" getting two vegetables in one. Try to select all beets of the same size for even cooking. Look for symmetrical shaping and a smooth surface. Older, large beets may be used but, due to their greater density, will take a long time to cook. They will lack the lively flavor of the younger roots. **93**

Preparation

Only the garden beet is considered here. For leaf beet (chard) look under greens. While it is necessary in conventional cooking to leave on the root and about 2 inches of the stems, in microwave oven cooking the stems and root may be cut off flush with the beet itself. There will be no bleeding of color as the beet is not cooked in a large quantity of water.

Take a stiff brush and scrub each beet, preferably under running water, to remove any dirt. Rinse well and it is ready to cook.

Cooking

Fresh

In some countries it is the custom for grocers to sell precooked beets; here, in the United States, it is necessary for you to cook your own. Actually, this is an advantage since you can control just how well done the beets are. Beets take a very long time to cook as they are very dense.

Arrange the beets in a casserole so that the larger beets are around the outer edges of the dish and the smaller ones in the middle, if this is possible. Add about 1 inch of water to the dish. Cover and cook in the microwave oven. Small beets take about 15 to 20 minutes to cook. Large beets can take up to 30 minutes to cook. Also, the amount of beets being cooked affects the time. When the side of the beet that is on the bottom begins to get tender, turn the beet over. It may be necessary to rearrange the beets to get more even cooking. If, as is often the case, the beets vary greatly in size, it may be necessary to remove each beet as it gets tender. As always, allow for the residual cooking so do not let the beet get quite as tender as you want it to be.

Dunk the beets in cold water just long enough to get them cool enough to handle for peeling. The skin of cooked beets practically slips off. Use a knife when and where it is necessary. Now the beet is ready to use any way you wish.

Frozen

94 Because beets are good keepers, they are not usually frozen.

Canned

Canned produce is fully cooked and only needs reheating.

Seasonings:	allspice, caraway, chives, fennel, garlic, ginger, lemon, onion, parsley, poppy seed, thyme, butter, salt, pepper, sugar, honey
Sauces:	Bearnaise, Garlic, Mornay, and Hot Orange sauces; sour cream; yogurt
Cheeses:	Cottage, Cream, Ricotta
Wines:	burgundy, claret, port, tokay
Nuts:	pumpkin seed, sunflower seed
Extra serving suggestions:	hot, with parsley sauce with 3 tablespoons minced chives added
	hot, with Béchamel sauce and 1 teaspoon crumbled tarragon and 1/4 teaspoon dry mustard added

QUICK HARVARD BEETS

Quick, because you use canned pickled beets, but with a touch of class because of the orange liqueur. If you don't tell, no one will guess how quick and easy it was.

Makes 4 servings   *Preparation time 10 Min.*

1   can (1 pound) pickled beets
3/4 cup liquid (beet juice plus water)
1   teaspoon sugar

1/2 teaspoon wine vinegar
1   tablespoon cornstarch
2   tablespoons Triple Sec liqueur
     Salt and pepper to taste

Drain the juice from the canned pickled beets into a measuring cup. Add enough water to bring it to 3/4 cup liquid. Mix the sugar, vinegar, cornstarch, and liqueur in a covered casserole. Gradually stir in the liquid. Cook, stirring once every 30 seconds until the mixture is thick and glossy, in the microwave oven. (This should take about 2 minutes.) Continue cooking for 2 or 3 minutes more on defrost or low power. If these powers are not available, let the sauce sit for 2 minutes and then cook 1 minute more on high.

95

Gently stir in the beets, salt, and pepper. Return to the microwave oven and heat, covered, until very hot. (This should take 3 to 4 minutes.)

Tip: Cointreau or other orange-flavored liqueur may be used in place of Triple Sec. Also, grated orange rind may be used by those who do not care to use liqueur. The alcohol does cook out leaving only the flavor of the liqueur.

My Time Is _____ *Min.*

BEETS À L'ORANGE

A slight touch of sweet and sour and the mandarin oranges make this a unique way to fix beets. They are tasty, colorful, and will surely appeal to children.

Makes 4 servings

- 1 tablespoon sugar
- 1 tablespoon cornstarch
- 1 teaspoon wine vinegar
- 1 pound cooked, diced beets

Preparation time 8 Min.

- 1 can (11 ounces) mandarin oranges
- Salt and pepper to taste

Mix the sugar, cornstarch, and vinegar in a casserole. Pour in the liquid from the mandarin oranges and gradually blend into the sugar-cornstarch mixture. Add the mandarin oranges and the diced beets. If using canned beets, do not use the liquid they are canned in unless it has been reduced to a few spoonfuls. Cook, covered, in the microwave oven until the mixture is hot and the liquid comes to a boil. It is very necessary to stir several times during the cooking period to thicken the liquid evenly. Continue cooking for 2 or 3 minutes more on defrost or low power. If these powers are not available, let the sauce sit for 2 minutes and then cook 1 minute more on high. Add salt and pepper to taste.

96

Tip: if using fresh beets, look back to the beginning of the chapter under *BEETS, Preparation* and *Cooking*. Follow the instructions there. For a flavor change, add 1/4 cup diced onion or scallion in with the mandarin oranges and beets.

My Time Is _____ Min.

RED BEET SALAD

This is a colorful salad, true, but see how easy it is to cook the beets in the microwave oven. There's no worry about the color bleeding and the flavor is all there.

Makes 4 servings   *Preparation time 25 Min.*

1 pound beets
1/4 cup water
3 tablespoons wine vinegar
1 tablespoon sugar
1/2 teaspoon salt
1/2 teaspoon caraway seed
1 tablespoon prepared horseradish
4 tablespoons mayonnaise

1 tablespoon capers (optional)
2 tablespoons chopped sweet pickle
1 hard-boiled egg, chopped (cooked conventionally)
2 tablespoons finely-chopped parsley

Cut the tops and the roots of the beets off flush with the beet root and discard. Put the beet root in a covered casserole with 1/4 cup water. Arrange the larger roots to the outside of the container and the smaller ones to the middle. Cook, covered, until tender (about 15 minutes). It may help to turn the beets over once about halfway through the cooking time, especially if they are quite mature. Cool. Peel and slice.

Combine the vinegar, sugar, salt, caraway seed, and horseradish. Pour over the beets and refrigerate at least 3 hours. Drain the beets and cut them into strips. Put them in the salad bowl. Combine the mayonnaise, capers, sweet pickle, and egg. Toss with the beets. Sprinkle on the chopped parsley and serve.

Tip: in microwave cooking the tops and roots can be cut off flush with the beet root because the beets are not being cooked in a large amount of water so there will be no "bleeding" of color. The color remains bright and clear.

My Time Is _____ Min.

TURKISH BEET SALAD

There are two beet salad recipes in this book. This one is the least exotic of the two and will, therefore, appeal to more tastes. When cooking the beets in the microwave oven, remember to turn them over halfway through for more even cooking. The smaller beets will need to be removed before the larger ones are done to prevent overcooking.

Makes 4 servings   *Preparation time 20 Min.*
3/4 pound beets   1 clove garlic, minced
1/3 cup water   Salt and pepper to taste
  1 tablespoon lemon juice   1 1/4 cups yogurt
  1 tablespoon olive or salad   2 tablespoons finely-
      oil   chopped parsley

Cut the beet tops and root off flush with the beet root. Put the beets and water in a covered casserole and cook in the microwave oven. Turn over halfway through the cooking period or whenever a beet starts to get soft on the underside. Cooking time should take from 15 to 18 minutes. Allow for residual cooking. Cool, peel, and dice. Mix the lemon juice and the oil. Blend in the garlic, salt, pepper, and yogurt. Fold in the beets. Chill well. Garnish with the chopped parsley.

98

Tip: the beets will not "bleed" or lose color when the tops and roots are cut off flush as the amount of water is so small in microwave cooking. You will retain all the color and the flavor.

My Time Is _____ Min.

BEET SALAD WITH YOGURT

Yogurt is fermented milk and has exactly the same food value as the milk from which it is made. It does have a lively, tangy flavor and has better keeping qualities than fresh milk. This method of keeping milk was developed in the hot region of the Eastern Mediterranean in the centuries before refrigeration was even dreamed of. Yogurt is also known as yoghurt and as madzoon. If you wish to make your own, add a small amount of yogurt to warm milk and let set in a warm place. The bacteria increase rapidly and in 8 to 12 hours you have yogurt. If the milk is pasteurized there is no need to pretreat it. If raw milk is being used, scald it and then cool it before using. Yogurt is used in many dishes in the Mediterranean areas and in south and central Europe. In recent years its use has spread through other parts of the world, as well.

Makes 4 servings	Preparation time 20 Min.
2 bunches beets (to make 2 or more cups diced)	2/3 cup low-fat yogurt
1/4 cup water	4 teaspoons lemon juice
2 teaspoons fennel seed	Salt and pepper to taste.

99

Put the beets and water in a covered casserole. Cook in the microwave oven until barely tender. Time varies with the size and amount of beets. Put the smaller beets in the center of the dish and the larger ones around the edge. Cool, peel, and dice.

Crush the fennel seed with a hammer. Mix the fennel, yogurt, lemon juice, salt, and pepper. Fold in the beets. Chill. Serve on a bed of lettuce leaves.

Tip: crush the fennel seed by putting in a plastic sandwich bag or between layers of cloth and pound with a hammer. The plastic is best as it does not absorb the oils released by the pounding. The finer the seeds are mashed, the more flavor is released.

My Time Is _____ Min.

BROCCOLI

Broccoli is a plant of the cabbage family. In the United States two distinct forms have been called broccoli. One was known as sprouting broccoli and is the one known today as broccoli. The other was known as heading broccoli or as cauliflower broccoli. Now it is called cauliflower. These plants are closely related to the cabbage but are milder in flavor. In both cases, the flower bud heads are the part that is eaten. The only other plant where the flower bud is eaten regularly is the artichoke.

Selection

Look for broccoli with heavy heads of tightly-closed buds. The stalks should be tender. Smell the broccoli. It should have a pleasant odor. If it smells strong or unpleasant, avoid it. Also avoid stalks that are too woody or that have the flower buds opening or turning yellow.

Preparation

Broccoli is a hard vegetable to cook as the stems are much more dense than the buds. It is just as difficult to cook conventionally as it is by microwave. Read on for some tips to make it easier.

If the broccoli is home grown it is best to soak it from 10 to 20 minutes in salted water to pull out any unwelcome guests. Afterwards, rinse in plain water.

If the vegetable is to be cooked whole, pare the heavier ends of the stems and cut off and discard the parts that are too tough to be desirable. Split the ends several times to make them cook faster. Splitting the ends allows more surfaces for the microwaves to enter into the broccoli so that it may cook faster.

If the broccoli is to be cooked in spears follow the same technique as above, except before splitting the stem ends, cut the vegetable into the desired spears. Then split the stem ends as seems necessary.

If the broccoli is to be cut into florets or pieces, pare the heavier ends of the stems and cut off and discard the parts that are too tough to eat. Then cut off the tender edible parts of the stems and cut into pieces or slices. Put aside. Break the tops into florets.

Cooking

Fresh

If the broccoli is to be cooked whole or in spears, use a rectangular or oval cooking dish. Put half the pieces with the butt ends to one side of the dish and the other half with the butt ends to the other end of the dish. Arrange so that the buds overlap each other. This will increase their functional density and slow down their cooking speed. Add 1/4 to 1/2 cup water. Cover and cook in the microwave oven until they are a bright green. Turn over, recover, and continue cooking until just barely tender. A single bunch weighing about 1 1/2 pounds will cook in 7 to 12 minutes. This great time span allows for differences in maturity, density, and in personal preferences for doneness. Allow for the residual cooking.

DO NOT USE FOIL IF YOUR OVEN DOES NOT ALLOW IT AS IT CAN CAUSE SEVERE DAMAGE TO SUCH OVENS, BUT *IF* YOUR OVEN WILL ALLOW THE USE OF FOIL (CHECK YOUR USE AND CARE MANUAL) you may also use this trick. When the spears are arranged as suggested and the dish is covered, in this case with plastic wrap so you can see what you are doing, wrap a strip of foil around the entire center of the dish so that the buds are covered but the stems are exposed. Cook until the stems are almost done. Then remove the foil and continue cooking until the buds are just barely tender. Allow for the residual cooking.

102

If the broccoli is to be cooked in florets, put 1/4 to 1/2 cup water in a baking dish. Add the stems and cook, covered, in the microwave oven until almost done. Add the florets. Stir. Cook, covered, stirring once or twice until the florets are just barely tender. (This should take about 5 to 8 minutes.)

Frozen

If in spears, cook, covered, in the microwave oven about 4 minutes to thaw. Separate and arrange with half of the spears with their butt ends to one end of the dish and the other half with their butt ends to the other end of the dish. Try to have the bud ends overlap. Continue cooking, covered, until barely tender. Allow for the residual cooking. (This should take about 3 to 5 minutes more for a 10-ounce package.)

If chopped or cut broccoli is being used, put it in a covered casserole and cook in the microwave oven, stirring twice, from 7 to 9 minutes or to the desired degree of doneness. Allow for the residual cooking.

Canned

Broccoli is not found canned but if it were, it would be fully cooked and only need reheating.

Seasonings:	dill, lemon, mint, nutmeg, onion, parsley, savory, sesame seed, thyme, butter, salt, pepper
Sauces:	Allemande, Bearnaise, Butter and Seed, Cheese, Garlic, Hollandaise, Hot Poppy, Mornay, and White sauces; sour cream
Cheeses:	American, Blue, Cheddar, Cream, Gorgonzola, Gruyère, Monterey Jack, Mozzarella, Parmesan, Provolone, Ricotta, Swiss
Wines:	chablis, rhine wine, sauterne, sherry, vermouth
Nuts:	almonds, pistachios, pumpkin seed, sunflower seed, water chestnuts
Extra serving suggestions:	hot, with sauce topped with toasted buttered bread crumbs
	hot, with sauce topped with crumbled bacon
	hot, with cream cheese thinned with lemon juice and with toasted almonds

NONI'S BROCCOLI-RICE BAKE

Noni Ohlsen, a neighbor, makes this casserole for both family and friends. All enjoy it very much. Here is a version converted to preparation in your microwave oven.

Makes 8 servings   *Preparation time 35 Min.*

- 2 packages frozen broccoli (10 ounces each)
- 1/4 cup water
- 1 1/4 cups rice
- 2 1/2 cups water
- 2 tablespoons butter or margarine
- 1/4 cup diced onion
- 1 can condensed cream of mushroom soup
- 1 can condensed cream of chicken soup
- 1 jar (8 ounces) processed cheese spread

Put the broccoli and 1/4 cup water in a covered casserole and cook in the microwave oven until just barely tender. Stir after 6 and 9 minutes respectively. The broccoli should cook in about 12 minutes. Set the broccoli aside.

104 In a very large, covered casserole mix the rice, water, butter, and onion. Cook, stirring several times, until tender (about 15 minutes). Add the broccoli, cream of mushroom soup, cream of chicken soup, and processed cheese spread. Mix thoroughly. Return to the microwave oven and heat, stirring several times more, until the mixture is hot through.

Tip: the broccoli-rice bake can make an excellent luncheon dish by the addition of cooked, slivered chicken. Alone, it provides both vegetable and starch.

My Time Is _____ *Min.*

POLYNESIAN-STYLE BROCCOLI

This is a stir-fry type of broccoli that is good, easy, and different. The broccoli retains its beautiful color cooked this way.

Makes 6 servings
1 bunch broccoli (about
      1 1/2 pounds)
1 tablespoon butter

Preparation time 15 Min.
1 clove garlic, minced
1 teaspoon salt

Wash and drain the broccoli. Cut the stems from the florets. Peel the stems and cut into 1/4-inch slices. Put the stems, butter, and garlic in a covered casserole and cook in the microwave oven, stirring several times, just until the stems become bright green. Cut the florets into 1/2-inch slices. Add to the casserole and continue cooking, covered, in the microwave, stirring from time to time, until the florets are bright green and just starting to get tender. Stir in the salt. Serve.

Tip: try other vegetables done in this manner. Some good choices would be asparagus, green beans, snow peas, and cabbage.

105

BRUSSELS SPROUTS

Brussels sprouts are relatives of the cabbage family. Instead of setting one head, many sprouts are formed along the stem like miniature heads of cabbage. It was grown in Belgium as early as 1587 and was named after the city of Brussels. Like all plants of the cabbage family, it is a cool weather crop. Thanks to the frozen food industry, Brussels sprouts are available the year around.

Selection

Look for firm-headed, medium bright green heads. If the outer leaves are yellowed, or if the heads are loose, the sprouts are past their prime. Also look for signs of worms. Commercially raised sprouts rarely have worms but those that do should be avoided. It is very important to select, if possible, sprouts that are all the same approximate size for even cooking. Small, medium, or large is a matter of personal preference. Having them all the same size makes it much easier to cook them evenly.

Preparation

Wash and drain the sprouts. Cut the stem-end back flush with the base of the head. Trim off any blemished or tough looking outer leaves.

Cooking

Fresh

Put the Brussels sprouts and 1/4 cup water in a covered casserole. Cook in the microwave oven, stirring at least 2 times, until tender. One pound of Brussels sprouts takes about 7 minutes to cook. One-and-a-half pounds takes about 9 to 10 minutes cooking time. Allow 5 minutes standing time.

Frozen

Put the frozen Brussels sprouts and 2 tablespoons water in a covered casserole and cook in the microwave, stirring twice to rearrange the sprouts, until tender. One 8-ounce package takes 6 to 8 minutes to cook and 2 packages take about 9 to 10 minutes to cook. Do not overcook but allow for the residual cooking during the standing time. Allow 3 to 5 minutes standing time.

Canned

Brussels sprouts do not come canned.

Seasonings:	basil, chives, curry, dill, lemon, onion, parsley, poppy seed, savory, sesame seed, thyme, butter, salt, pepper
Sauces:	Allemande, Béchamel, Butter and Seed, Cheese, Hollandaise, Hot Poppy Seed, Mornay, Velouté, and White sauces; sour cream
Cheeses:	American, Cheddar, Cream, Gruyère, Monterey Jack, Mozzarella, Parmesan, Provolone, Romano, Swiss
Wines:	chablis, rhine wine, sauterne, sherry, dry vermouth
Nuts:	almonds, pumpkin seed, sunflower seed, water chestnuts
Extra serving suggestions:	hot, with White sauce mixed with basil, onion, and parsley
	hot, with cheese sauce mixed with chablis wine and dill weed
	hot, with butter, lemon juice, and toasted almonds

CURRIED BRUSSELS SPROUTS

The colors of the Brussels sprouts, the sauce, and the bacon make as good a combination as the flavors. Here is a recipe that will cure the Brussels sprouts blahs.

Makes 4 servings　　　　　　　　　*Preparation time 18 Min.*

2 slices bacon	1/2 teaspoon curry powder
1 pound Brussels sprouts	1/2 teaspoon salt
1/4 cup water	1 teaspoon instant minced
2 tablespoons butter or	onion
margarine	1 cup milk
2 tablespoons flour	

Put the bacon on several layers of paper toweling and cook in the microwave oven until well browned (about 2 minutes). Remove and set aside. While the bacon is cooking, wash and prepare the sprouts. Put the sprouts and 1/4 cup water in a covered casserole. Cook in the microwave oven, stirring twice, until barely tender (about 7 minutes). Remove and set aside.

Melt the butter in a small dish or casserole in the microwave oven. Stir in the flour, curry powder, salt, and instant onion. **109** Blend in the milk. Cook, stirring once every minute, until the mixture thickens and comes to a boil in the microwave oven. Continue cooking for 2 or 3 minutes more on defrost or low power. If these powers are not available, let the sauce sit for 2 minutes and then cook 1 minute more on high. Crumble the bacon finely. Pour the sauce and bacon over the sprouts and stir gently to coat each sprout. Serve.

Tip: if your family doesn't like hot seasonings, decrease the curry powder to 1/4 teaspoon. The flavor is better at the higher level.

My Time Is _____ *Min.*

BRUSSELS SPROUTS PARMESAN

This time you are in a hurry. You don't want anything complicated, yet you don't want to sacrifice flavor. This is the recipe for you, but don't reserve it only for when you are rushed.

Makes 4 servings   *Preparation time 15 Min.*

1   pound Brussels sprouts or   2   tablespoons butter
     2 8-ounce packages   1/4 cup grated Parmesan
     frozen sprouts   cheese
1/4 cup water (2 tablespoons   Salt and pepper to taste
     for frozen sprouts)

Put the Brussels sprouts, water, and butter in a covered casserole. Cook in the microwave oven, stirring twice, until tender. Fresh sprouts will take about 7 minutes cooking time. Frozen ones cook in 9 to 10 minutes.

Drain the liquid from the sprouts into a small dish or casserole. Reduce by boiling in the microwave oven until only the butter remains. Pour over the sprouts.

110 Add the Parmesan cheese, salt, and pepper. Stir to coat each sprout evenly.

Tip: if you like the flavor of garlic in the above recipe, cook 1 clove finely-minced garlic in the butter for 1 minute. Add the Brussels sprouts and water and continue as above.

My Time Is _____ *Min.*

SWEET AND SOUR BRUSSELS SPROUTS

Something a bit different for Brussels sprouts that will get you repeat calls. If using frozen sprouts, use 2 8-ounce packages in place of the fresh ones.

Makes 4 servings		*Preparation time 20 Min.*
4 slices bacon		2 teaspoons wine vinegar
1 pound Brussels sprouts		2 teaspoons sugar
1/4 cup water		Salt and pepper to taste
2 tablespoons butter or margarine		

Cook the bacon on paper toweling in the microwave oven until brown (about 4 minutes). Set aside.

Put the Brussels sprouts and water in a covered casserole. Cook in the microwave oven, stirring after 4 and 6 minutes cooking time respectively, until tender (about 7 minutes). Drain the liquid into a small dish. Set the Brussels sprouts aside.

111

Add the butter, vinegar, and sugar to the Brussels sprouts liquid. Cook until the butter melts, the sugar can be dissolved by stirring, and until most of the liquid has boiled away.

Crumble the bacon. Add it and the butter mixture, salt, and pepper to the Brussels sprouts. Stir gently to coat each sprout with the butter mixture. Serve.

Tip: 1/4 cup chopped onion, cooked in with the sprouts, would make a nice flavor change. For a bit of color add some strips of pimiento.

My Time Is _____ *Min.*

CABBAGE

The food cabbages are a varied lot and sometimes it is surprising to find a certain plant is actually a cabbage. Of the plants we eat, all of these are cabbages; kale, collards, common cabbage, savoy cabbage, Brussels sprouts, broccoli, cauliflower, and kohlrabi.

Kale has a rosette of leaves formed around its stem. In the United States, usually the whole stem is cut off for harvesting. In Europe, the leaves are harvested individually so that a longer crop season is obtained. Cold weather improves kale so it is usually grown as a fall green when other greens are long gone. This trait is not as important as it once was as many forms of greens are now available the year around.

Collards is another form of loose-leafed cabbage. The leaves are broader than those of kale and look more like cabbage leaves. The leaves may be picked progressively, as they mature, or the whole plant may be cut off and harvested at one time.

Brussels sprouts is discussed in the Brussels sprouts section of this book.

Broccoli is discussed in the Broccoli section of this book. **113**

Cauliflower is discussed in the Cauliflower section of this book.

Cabbage, hard-head cabbage like the cannon ball type was developed in Northern Europe. Soft-headed types, such as Savoy, were developed in Southern Europe. All cabbages are cool weather crops. The firm, dense heads are the type suitable for long-term storage. Sauerkraut is a form of cabbage that has been fermented in a salt brine.

Selection

Look for firm, heavy heads of clear color whether you are buying green or red cabbage. If the leaves are yellowed, wilted, or marred, do not buy. If the outer leaves are not large but rather appear like the inner leaves do, it means the head has been held a long time and trimmed back to make it look fresh.

Preparation

Rinse and drain the head of cabbage. Trim off any tough or damaged outer leaves. Cut the stem even with the head. The head may be cooked whole, cut in wedges, sliced, or chopped.

Cooking

Fresh

Fresh is the only way cabbage comes, with the exception of sauerkraut, which is a form of fermented cabbage. A whole head of cabbage may be wrapped in wax paper or plastic wrap and cooked in its own steam. A medium-sized head will take about 12 to 15 minutes. If you are making stuffed cabbage leaves, the leaves can be softened this way and then removed from the head. The center of the head can be reserved and used in another dish.

Cabbage cut into wedges should be put in a covered casserole with 2 tablespoons of water to cook in the microwave oven. The wedges should be rearranged at the end of each 4 minutes of cooking time. A 1 1/2-pound head of cabbage cut into wedges takes about 9 to 10 minutes to cook. A 2-pound head should take 10 to 12 minutes.

Cabbage cut into thin slices or chopped usually needs no water added as there are enough ruptured cells exposed to give off enough water for the cooking process. Put it into a covered casserole, stir after 3 and 5 minutes respectively for even cooking. Four cups chopped cabbage will cook in 5 to 6 minutes while 8 cups will take 8 to 9 minutes.

114

Seasonings:	caraway, celery seed, cumin (comino), dill, fennel, horseradish, lemon, mustard, onion, paprika, parsley, poppy seed, savory, sesame seed, thyme, butter, salt, pepper, sugar, honey
Sauces:	Allemande, Butter and Seed, Cheese, Hot Poppy Seed, and Mornay sauces; sour cream
Cheeses:	American, Cheddar, Monterey Jack, Swiss
Wine:	sauterne
Nuts:	pumpkin seed, sunflower seed, water chestnuts
Extra serving suggestions:	hot, with White sauce or Velouté sauce seasoned with poppy seed and horseradish
	hot, with salt, pepper, butter, and caraway seed
	hot, with sugar, lemon juice, butter, and caraway

CABBAGE HAWAIIAN

The pineapple and sugar give a slight sweet and sour taste to Cabbage Hawaiian and the toasted coconut gives a bit of crunch. The overall effect is delightful.

Makes 4 servings   *Preparation time 10 Min.*

1 1/2	pounds cabbage
3	tablespoons butter
3	teaspoons sugar
6	tablespoons canned crushed pineapple, juice included
1/4	cup toasted coconut

Cut the head of cabbage in half, lengthwise. Cut the cabbage in wedges and remove the core. Stack two wedges together so that the thin side of one wedge of cabbage is on the thick side of a second wedge. Slice thinly. Repeat until all the cabbage is sliced. Put the cabbage, butter, sugar, and pineapple in a covered casserole. Stir. Cook in the microwave oven, stirring once, until tender (about 7 minutes). Stir in the coconut and serve.

115

Tip: coconut toasts beautifully in the microwave oven but needs very frequent stirring to prevent burning in spots. Toast a whole package of coconut at one time. Store in an air-tight container and you have toasted coconut for whenever you want it.

My Time Is _____ Min.

NORWEGIAN CABBAGE WITH SOUR CREAM

Tasty, different, and utterly delicious, try this recipe in place of the usual boiled cabbage. It is a winner.

Makes 6 servings   *Preparation time 15 Min.*

1 medium-small head of cabbage, shredded	1/2 teaspoon pepper
1/4 cup water	2/3 cup sour cream (or a bit more)
1 1/2 teaspoons salt	1 tablespoon dill weed

Wash and trim any tough outer leaves from the cabbage. Shred it finely, until you have about 4 cups shredded cabbage. Put the cabbage and water in a covered casserole and cook in the microwave oven, stirring several times, until the cabbage is tender-crisp (about 7 to 8 minutes). Stir together the salt, pepper, sour cream, and dill weed. Mix into the hot cabbage. Cook, covered, 1 minute more.

116 **Tip:** do not overcook the cabbage during the first stage, as there will be 1 minute more of cooking plus the residual cooking. The cabbage should still have some crispness left to it for texture. The amount of crispness will depend upon individual preference.

My Time Is _____ Min.

POPPY SEED CABBAGE

For a rich flavor plus the crunch of the poppy seed try Poppy Seed Cabbage. It is amazing how a few simple things make a run-of-the-mill dish into a treat.

Makes 4 servings	Preparation time 15 Min.
3 slices bacon, diced	2 teaspoons poppy seed
1/4 cup chopped onion	Salt and pepper to taste
1 1/2 pounds cabbage, coarsely chopped	

Cook the bacon in a casserole in the microwave oven, stirring twice, until crisp and brown. Remove the bacon with a slotted spoon and reserve.

Add the onions to the bacon fat. Cook, covered, in the microwave oven for 3 minutes. Add the cabbage. Cook, covered, in the microwave oven, stirring twice, until barely tender (about 6 to 7 minutes). Add the bacon, poppy seed, salt, and pepper. Stir to mix well. Let stand 5 minutes before serving.

Tip: for a change of flavor substitute sesame seed or celery seed **117** for the poppy seed. If using the celery seed, cut back on the amount used as it is more strongly flavored.

My Time Is _____ Min.

SWEET AND SOUR CABBAGE

What could be more traditional to Central Europe than this colorful, flavorful concoction? It makes an eye-appealing accent, as well as an appetizing addition to any meal.

Makes 6 servings   *Preparation time 25 Min.*

3	slices bacon, diced	1/8	teaspoon pepper
1/4	cup chopped onion	1/4	cup brown sugar, packed
2	tablespoons flour	6	cups finely-chopped red cabbage
3	tablespoons vinegar		
1/4	cup water	1	teaspoon caraway seed (optional)
1	teaspoon salt		

Put the bacon and onion in a covered casserole and cook in the microwave oven 5 minutes. Stir in the flour and then the vinegar and water. Add the salt, pepper, and sugar and stir. Add the cabbage and caraway seed and stir well to coat the cabbage evenly. Cook, covered, in the microwave oven for 8 to 10 minutes, stirring several times. Add enough water to almost cover the cabbage and cook several minutes more to heat through.

118 **Tip:** the cabbage should have some texture and crispness left. How much crispness depends upon your preference. Remember, the longer cabbage is cooked, the more the strong (often objectionable) cabbage flavor and odor are developed. The quick cooking of the microwave oven allows cabbage to be naturally sweet. If you prefer a sweeter, less sharp flavor to the dish, add more sugar or use slightly less vinegar.

My Time Is _____ *Min.*

CARROT

The carrot is an herbacious biennial plant. That means it usually flowers and sets seed the second year (biennial) and that the leaves die down to the ground during the winter and come up from the root in the spring. It is the root of the plant that is eaten. In some areas the root is left in the ground for winter storage and then a supply is dug up from time-to-time when the ground thaws.

The carrot is native to Afghanistan and was known before the Christian era began. It was grown in China by the 1200's. The plant is most valued as a precursor of vitamin A, that means the human body can take carotene and convert it into vitamin A.

In the United States, the orange-colored carrot is usually grown. There are, however, carrots with orange, white-yellow, and purple flesh as well as varieties with orange, red, and purple skins.

Selection

Look for carrots that are smooth, young, and have good coloring. Smooth carrots will have less waste in the paring or scraping. Avoid carrots that are rough, limp, slit, or old looking. The older a carrot is the longer it will need to cook. If the carrots are to be cooked whole, select them to be a uniform size for even cooking.

Preparation

Wash the carrots. Very dirty ones may need the use of a vegetable brush. Whether to pare, scrape, or leave the peel on is usually a matter of personal preference. Leaving the peel on is good from the nutrition point but often gives a stronger flavor to the carrots.

Cooking

Fresh

When cooking the carrots whole, except for the tiny ones, use a rectangular cooking dish like a loaf dish. Lay half the carrots with the thick top end to one end of the dish. Lay the other half with their thick top ends to the other end of the dish. Try to have the slender ends overlap. Add 1/4 cup water and cover with plastic wrap or wax paper. Cook in the microwave oven until tender. (This should take about 8 to 12 minutes.) Rearranging is necessary halfway through the cooking time. Mentally divide the dish into quarters. Turn each quarter over so that the carrots that were in the center of the dish are now on the outside of the dish.

When cooking the carrots that are cut up, or if using tiny whole ones, put them in a covered casserole with 1/4 cup water. Cook in the microwave oven stirring twice during the cooking period. One pound of carrots will take 7 to 10 minutes.

Frozen

For whole tiny frozen carrots put 8 ounces of carrots and 2 tablespoons water in a covered casserole. Cook in the microwave oven until tender, about 6 minutes. Stir after 4 minutes of cooking.

For cut up carrots, put 10 ounces of carrots and 2 tablespoons water in a covered casserole. Cook in the microwave oven until tender (about 8 to 10 minutes). Stir after 4 and 6 minutes of cooking respectively.

Canned

120 Canned carrots are already cooked and only need reheating to be ready to use.

Seasonings:	basil, caraway, dill, fennel, ginger, lemon, marjoram, mint, nutmeg, onion, parsley, poppy seed, sesame seed, butter, salt, pepper, sugar, honey, molasses
Sauces:	Allemande, Bearnaise, Béchamel, Butter and Seed, Hollandaise, Hot Orange, Hot Poppy Seed, Velouté, and White sauces; French dressing; yogurt
Cheeses:	Cream, Swiss
Wines:	chablis, rhine wine, rosé, sauterne, sherry, tokay, dry vermouth, sweet vermouth
Nuts:	pistachios, pumpkin seed, sunflower seed, water chestnuts
Extra serving suggestions:	hot, with butter, chopped mint leaves, salt, and pepper hot, with brown sugar, butter, and nutmeg cold, with French dressing and chopped parsley

CARROTS WITH ANISE

This is a novel and interesting way to fix carrots. Not only is this dish high in vitamin A, but it is also high in vitamin C. The taste of anise is a bit like licorice. Another time, try substituting fennel for anise for a slightly different taste.

Makes 4 servings	*Preparation time 20 Min.*
1 pound carrots	1/4 cup orange juice
1/4 cup water	1 tablespoon snipped
2 tablespoons butter	parsley
1/2 teaspoon anise seed,	Salt and pepper to taste
crushed	

Scrape carrots; cut diagonally into 1/2-inch slices. Cook, covered, in a 1-quart casserole with 1/4 cup water until almost tender (about 12 minutes). Allow for the residual cooking effect of the microwave oven on vegetables. It is essential to stir carrots several times during cooking in the microwave oven, to obtain even cooking. Place the butter and the crushed anise seed in a small dish and cook 2 minutes in the microwave oven. Add to the carrots. Stir in the orange juice, parsley, salt, and pepper. Cook in the microwave oven a minute or two longer, to heat through.

121

Tip: do not add salt to carrots during their initial cooking, as it is apt to toughen them. If too much water remains after the cooking, substitute 1 tablespoon frozen concentrate of orange juice for the regular-strength orange juice. To crush the seed, place in a small sandwich bag or between sheets of plastic wrap or wax paper and pound with a hammer or other flat-surfaced, heavy object. Crushing releases the oils of flavoring agents. Cooking with the butter permeates the butter with the other flavors.

My Time Is _____ Min.

CRAZY CREAMY CARROTS

The rich, creamy sauce flavored with onion and nutmeg makes these carrots so good you will think you are having dessert. But don't let that fool you. They really are carrots, but after eating them, maybe you won't want dessert.

Makes 6 servings　　　　　　　　*Preparation time 18 Min.*

- 1　pound carrots, pared and sliced
- 1/4　cup chopped onion
- 1/4　cup water
- 2　tablespoons butter or margarine
- 2　tablespoons flour
- 1　cup light cream (half and half)
- 1/4　teaspoon nutmeg
- Salt and pepper to taste

Put the carrots, onion, and water in a covered casserole. Cook, stirring after 4 and 6 minutes respectively, in the microwave oven until tender (about 7 to 9 minutes). Drain the liquid from the carrots into a 1-quart covered casserole. Set the carrots aside.

122 To the carrot water, add the butter. Cook, uncovered, in the microwave oven until the water is evaporated and only the butter remains. Stir in the flour. Slowly blend in the cream. Add the nutmeg, salt, and pepper. Cook, covered, stirring every 1 1/2 minutes until the sauce thickens and comes to a boil. Continue cooking 2 or 3 minutes more on defrost or low power. If these powers are not available, let the sauce sit for 2 minutes and then cook 1 minute more on high. Add the sauce to the carrots. Serve.

Tip: the reason for adding the carrot water to the butter and then reducing it (boiling off the water), is to save any nutrients that may have found their way into the water. Try this trick with any vegetables that have butter on them.

My Time Is _____ Min.

CARROT GOLD

The taste of these carrots is to the epicure as the sight of gold was to the Forty-Niners. The blending of flavors is delightful.

Makes 4 servings

1	pound carrots
1/4	cup water
1/4	cup chopped onion
2	tablespoons butter margarine
2	tablespoons flour

Preparation time 25 Min.

1	tablespoon sugar
1/4	teaspoon nutmeg
2	tablespoons sherry wine (optional)
1	cup milk
2	egg yolks

Pare and slice the carrots. Put the carrots and water in a covered casserole. Cook in the microwave oven, stirring once, until tender (about 8 minutes). Set the carrots aside.

Put the onions and butter in a small dish or casserole. Cook, covered, 3 minutes. Blend in the flour, sugar, and nutmeg. Stir in the wine. Gradually stir in the milk. Cook in the microwave oven, stirring once every few minutes, until the mixture thickens and comes to a boil. Put the sauce and the carrots in a blender. Blend just long enough to chop up the carrots and blend the mixture. **123** Put the egg yolks on the bottom of the carrot casserole. Gradually blend in some of the carrot mixture, then stir in the rest.

Return to the microwave oven. Cook, covered, 2 minutes. Very carefully, using a large spoon, stir the carrot mixture so that the outer parts are brought to the center of the dish and the center part is taken to the outer edge of the dish. Cook, covered, 2 minutes more. Let stand 5 minutes. Serve.

Tip: if you want to make this into a dessert, sweeten to taste instead of using the 1 tablespoon sugar. This will make an excellent carrot pudding.

My Time Is _____ Min.

MINTED HONEY CARROTS

"Fixing" fine vegetables is so easy in the microwave oven there is little excuse for not making them special. Minted honey carrots are special and take next to no time to fix.

Makes 4 servings   *Preparation time 13 Min.*

1 pound carrots, pared and sliced	1/4 cup water
1/4 teaspoon dried mint leaves, crumbled fine	3 tablespoons honey
	1 tablespoon butter or margarine

Put the carrots, mint, and water in a covered casserole. Cook in the microwave oven, stirring after 4 and 6 minutes of cooking, until the carrots are tender (about 7 minutes). Drain the liquid from the carrots into a small bowl or casserole. Set the carrots aside.

To the carrot water, add the honey and butter. Cook, uncovered, in the microwave oven until the mixture is as thick as a medium syrup. Stir the syrup into the carrots. Serve.

124 **Tip:** if fresh mint is used, mince it very, very fine. In general, when substituting fresh herbs for dried ones in recipes, use four times as much of the fresh herb.

My Time Is _____ Min.

CARROTS IN MILK

Celantro, the seasoning used with this carrot dish, is the plant from which coriander seeds are obtained. Try to find it in your Mexican or Oriental specialty shops.

Makes 6 servings   *Preparation time 20 Min.*

8 large carrots, peeled and sliced very thin	2 tablespoons butter
1/4 cup water	2 tablespoons minced celantro or parsley
1 teaspoon sugar	1/2 teaspoon salt
1/8 teaspoon pepper	1 cup milk

Put the carrots, water, sugar, pepper, butter, and celantro in a covered 1 1/2-quart casserole and cook until the carrots are tender. In the microwave oven, this can take from 8 to 15 minutes, depending upon the age and tenderness of the carrots. The older and more mature they are, the longer the cooking time. Stir several times during the cooking period for even cooking. When the carrots are tender, add the salt and milk. Heat to a simmer and serve.

Tip: if you can't find fresh celantro, you can use 1/2 teaspoon **125** dried celantro. If celantro is unavailable in your area, substitute the parsley.

My Time Is _____ Min.

COPPER PENNY SALAD

Here is a delightful recipe from my friend Joyce Raney. She says the recipe has been in her family for years. It is certain that once you have tasted it, it will be a favorite of your family for years, too.

Makes 8 servings

- 2 pounds carrots
- 1/3 cup water
- 1 cup sugar
- 1/2 cup salad oil
- 1 teaspoon salt
- 1/2 teaspoon pepper

Preparation time 20 Min.

- 1/2 teaspoon dry mustard
- 1/4 cup chopped green pepper
- 1/4 cup chopped onion
- 1 can tomato soup

Prepare and slice the carrots. Put the carrots and the water in a covered casserole. Cook in the microwave oven, stirring twice, until the carrots are almost tender enough. (This will take about 12 to 20 minutes.) Drain and set aside.

126 Mix all the other ingredients in a small, covered casserole. Heat and stir the sauce until the sugar is thoroughly dissolved. Pour over the carrots. Stir again. Let marinate at least 8 hours or overnight.

Tip: allow for the residual cooking in judging the doneness of the carrots so that they will not be too soft. Marinating is necessary to allow the flavors to penetrate into the carrots. Cooking time is greatly affected by the maturity of the carrots.

My Time Is _____ Min.

CARROT PUDDING

Try this delicious carrot pudding from India that, if done conventionally, would take 2 hours, but takes only 40 minutes in the microwave oven.

Makes 6 servings	Preparation time 40 Min.
1/2 cup blanched almonds	3 cups milk
4 cups grated carrots	1/2 teaspoon vanilla
1/2 cup currants	2 tablespoons heavy cream
1/4 cup sugar	1 lime or lemon cut in
1/2 stick cinnamon	wedges

Chop the almonds medium-fine. Mix 1/2 of the nuts, the carrots, currants, sugar, cinnamon, and milk in a large, covered casserole. Cook, covered, in the microwave oven until the mixture comes to a boil. Continue cooking, uncovered, until the milk is absorbed and/or evaporated away. Stir from time-to-time during the cooking. Stir in the vanilla and the cream. Chop the remaining nuts very fine and sprinkle over the top of the pudding. Chill. Serve with lime or lemon wedges to be squeezed over the pudding.

127

Tip: use up your older, more mature carrots for this pudding. Save the younger, more tender ones for other recipes.

My Time Is _____ Min.

CAULIFLOWER

Cauliflower, like broccoli, is a plant of the cabbage family. In the United States two distinct forms have been called broccoli. One was known as sprouting broccoli and is the one known today as broccoli. The other was known as heading broccoli or as cauliflower broccoli and is now called simply cauliflower. These plants are closely related to the cabbage but are milder in flavor. In both cases, the flower bud heads are the part that is eaten. The other plant where the flower bud is eaten regularly is the artichoke.

Selection

Look for firm, compact, creamy white heads of cauliflower. Check the leaves around the head. Are they fresh and firm? Avoid heads with blemishes and brown spots, if possible. Wilted, yellowed leaves are another sign that the head is past its peak.

Preparation

Trim off any excess leaves. A few very small green leaves may be left on for color contrast. If the cauliflower is home grown or grown organically without the use of pesticides, soak it for about 10 to 20 minutes in salt water. This will help to pull out any unwelcome guests that may have set up housekeeping in the head. (Ordinarily this step is not needed with commercially grown products.) Next, rinse under running water. If the cauliflower is to be cooked whole, try to cut out as much of the core as is convenient without allowing it to fall to pieces. If it is to be cooked in florets, divide the head into the florets and cut off any excess core that is not to be eaten.

Cooking

Fresh

If the cauliflower is to be cooked whole, wrap it in either wax paper or plastic wrap and cook in the microwave oven until it is almost as tender as desired (allow for the residual cooking). Let stand 5 minutes before serving. A whole head of cauliflower takes from 6 to 9 minutes to cook depending both on the size and the density.

If the cauliflower is to be cooked in florets, place them in a casserole with 1/4 cup water. Cover and cook until almost tender. It is essential to stir gently at least 2 times during the cooking process. Let stand 5 minutes before serving. Allow from 6 to 9 minutes cooking time depending on the size and the density of the head.

Frozen

One has no choice but to cook frozen cauliflower in the florets as that is the only way it comes. Put it in a covered casserole and cook it in the microwave oven until almost tender. Stir it gently twice during the cooking time for even cooking. A 10-ounce package, the usual size, takes from 4 to 6 minutes to cook.

Canned

Normally cauliflower does not come canned. If it did, it would be fully cooked and only need reheating.

Seasonings:	caraway, chervil, coriander, dill, lemon, marjoram, onion, parsley, poppy seed, rosemary, sesame seed, thyme, butter, salt, pepper
Sauces:	Allemande, Béchamel, Butter and Seed, Cheese, Hollandaise, Hot Poppy Seed, Mornay, Parsley, Tomato, Velouté, and White sauces; French dressing
Cheeses:	American, Blue, Cheddar, Cream, Gorgonzola, Gruyère, Monterey Jack, Parmesan, Romano, Stilton
Wines:	chablis, rhine wine, sauterne, dry vermouth
Nuts:	almonds, sunflower seed, water chestnuts
Extra serving suggestions:	hot, with Mornay sauce made with Gruyère cheese and a little sauterne wine
	hot, with a mixture of mayonnaise, spicy brown mustard, and minced onion and topped with grated cheddar cheese
	cold, with French dressing
	raw, with a dip of mayonnaise, garlic, lemon juice, and dill weed to taste

CHEESY SAUCE CAULIFLOWER

Cauliflower fixed this way can be a delight in itself or it can be the center of a vegetable tray. One person, who does not like cauliflower, said of the recipe "Be sure and give that one to my Mom. I'll eat it."

Makes 4 to 6 servings　　　　　　*Preparation time 10 Min.*

- 1 head of cauliflower
- 1/4 cup finely-chopped onion
- 1 teaspoon butter or margarine
- 6 tablespoons milk or cream
- 3 ounces Cream cheese or Neufchatel cheese
- 1 1/2 teaspoons spicy brown mustard (more, if you like)
- 1/4 cup chopped parsley

Cut off the leaves on the head of cauliflower. Cut out an inverted cone of the core but do not break up the head. Wrap in plastic wrap or wax paper and cook until barely tender in the microwave oven (about 6 to 8 minutes).

Put the onion and butter in a small, covered casserole and cook 2 minutes in the microwave oven. Add the milk and Cream cheese. **131** Cook 1 minute and stir to blend. Cook 1 minute more and stir to finish blending. Stir in the mustard.

Place the head of cauliflower in a serving dish. Spoon the sauce over the head and let it run down the sides. Garnish with the chopped parsley.

Tip: leave on a few of the very tiny inner leaves of the cauliflower for a color contrast. They turn a beautiful shade of green.

My Time Is _____ Min.

CURRIED CAULIFLOWER #1

Cauliflower is so good in the microwave oven, but this sauce adds a little extra something. You are certain to enjoy it.

Makes 6 servings
- 1 teaspoon butter
- 1/4 cup bread or corn flake crumbs
- 1 medium head of cauliflower
- 1/4 cup water
- 1 tablespoon butter

Preparation time 20 Min.
- 1 tablespoon plus 1 teaspoon flour
- 1 teaspoon curry powder (more or less)
- 1/2 teaspoon salt
- 1/2 cup chopped sweet pickle
- 1 cup milk

Mix the teaspoon of butter and the crumbs in a small dish and toast in the microwave oven, stirring often to prevent uneven browning or burning. When nicely toasted, set aside.

Wash the cauliflower and break into florets. Put in a covered casserole with the water. Cook, covered, in the microwave oven, stirring a time or two, until the cauliflower is barely tender. (This should take 6 to 8 minutes.) Set aside.

132

In another casserole, or a 4-cup measure, melt the butter in the microwave oven. Stir in the flour and then the curry powder and salt. Mix in the sweet pickle. Gradually blend in the milk. Cook, stirring several times, in the microwave oven until the sauce thickens and comes to a boil. Pour over the cauliflower and stir gently. Sprinkle on the toasted crumbs and cook, covered, in the microwave oven another minute or two to reheat the cauliflower. Do not stir.

Tip: for a richer sauce, substitute light or heavy cream for the milk. If you like hot seasoning, add more curry powder. If you are sensitive to hot seasoning, try only 1/2 teaspoon.

My Time Is _____ Min.

CURRIED CAULIFLOWER #2

Spark up and pretty up cauliflower in one operation. Try this for family or friends. You will be glad you did.

Makes 4 servings

- 2 slices bacon
- 1 medium head of cauliflower
- 2 tablespoons butter or margarine
- 2 tablespoons flour

Preparation time 18 Min.

- 1/2 teaspoon curry powder
- 1/2 teaspoon salt
- 1 teaspoon instant minced onion
- 1 cup milk

Put the bacon on several layers of paper toweling and cook in the microwave oven until well browned (about 2 minutes). Remove and set aside. While the bacon is cooking, wash and prepare the cauliflower. Wrap the cauliflower in wax paper and cook in the microwave oven until tender (about 6 to 8 minutes). Remove and set aside.

Melt the butter in a small dish or casserole in the microwave oven. Stir in the flour, curry powder, salt, and instant onion. Blend in the milk. Cook, stirring once every minute, until the mixture thickens and comes to a boil. Continue cooking for 2 or 3 minutes on defrost or low power. If these powers are not available, let the sauce sit for 2 minutes and then cook 1 minute more on high. Crumble the bacon finely. Stir 3/4 of the bacon into the sauce. **133**

Put the cauliflower on a serving dish. Pour over the sauce. Sprinkle on the rest of the crumbled bacon. Serve.

Tip: if you are using frozen cauliflower or cauliflower that has been cut into florets, cook them until medium-tender in a casserole. Pour over the sauce and garnish as above.

My Time Is _____ Min.

CAULIFLOWER AND EGGPLANT IN PARMESAN SAUCE

Try this dish that incorporates two vegetables rarely put into the same recipe in this country. It takes a few minutes to put this together, but it will be worth the time.

Makes 6 servings   *Preparation time 35 Min.*

1	medium eggplant	2	tablespoons flour
	Salt		Salt and pepper to taste
1	medium head of		Dash of cayenne
	cauliflower	1/2	cup milk
1/4	cup water	1/2	cup light cream
2	tablespoons butter	1/2	cup grated Parmesan
	Salt and pepper to taste		cheese
1/4	cup butter		

Peel the eggplant and cut into 1/4-inch thick slices. Salt and put on paper toweling to pull out any bitter juices. Break the head of cauliflower into florets. Place them with 1/4 cup water in a covered casserole and cook in the microwave oven until almost tender. (This should require about 5 minutes.) Rinse the salt from the eggplant and pat dry with paper toweling. Melt the 2 tablespoons butter in a 2-quart rectangular baking dish (12″ × 9″). Put in the eggplant in a single layer and turn over to coat both sides with butter. Cover and cook in the microwave oven until almost tender (about 5 minutes). Put the cauliflower on top of the eggplant and sprinkle on the salt and pepper.

134

In another container, make the sauce. Melt 1/4 cup butter in a small, covered container. Blend in the flour, salt, pepper, and cayenne, then the milk and cream. Cook, covered, in the microwave oven until thick, about 3 minutes, stirring at the end of each minute. When the sauce has thickened and come to a boil, cook it for 2 minutes more on defrost or low power. If these powers are not available, let the sauce sit for 2 minutes and then cook 1 minute more on high. Stir in the Parmesan cheese. Pour over the vegetables, coating as evenly as possible. Cover, return to the microwave oven, and cook 2 minutes more. Let stand 3 minutes before serving.

Tip: be careful not to overcook. Vegetables are best when they still retain enough crispness to have some texture to them.

My Time Is _____ *Min.*

NORWEGIAN COLD CAULIFLOWER WITH SHRIMP

This dish is excellent to serve on a hot day or as part of a smorgasbord. Cook long enough in advance to chill thoroughly.

Makes 6 servings
1 large head of cauliflower
1 1/2 cups mayonnaise
1 pound cold cooked, shelled shrimp
1 hard-boiled egg, shelled and sliced (cooked conventionally)

Preparation time 15 Min.
Parsley sprigs
Olives and pimiento strips (optional)
Tomato or beet slices (optional)

Trim and wash the head of cauliflower. Wrap it in wax paper and cook it in the microwave oven until it is almost tender. (This should take about 8 to 9 minutes.) Leave it wrapped in the wax paper and chill.

When ready to serve, beat the mayonnaise until smooth and spread over the cauliflower. Arrange the shrimp in a decorative design. Garnish with the hard-boiled egg slices and the parsley sprigs. For more festive occasions, garnish more elaborately with the other suggested garnishes.

135

Tip: if the cauliflower is cooked until it is as tender as you like, it will be overcooked, as there is more residual cooking in microwave cooking than in conventional cooking. For a change of pace, a little powdered onion beaten into the mayonnaise with a touch of mustard makes a nice added touch. Do not try to cook an egg in the shell in the microwave oven. If you have no other cooking appliance and if your oven will tolerate foil, the eggs can be wrapped in foil and placed in a container with water to cover. They will take as long to cook this way as they will when cooked conventionally.

My Time Is _____ *Min.*

CELERY AND CELERIAC

The celery family gives us three food products; celery, celeriac, and celery seed. It was first found around the Eastern Mediterranean area. It was used only as a flavoring or in folk medicine. The first record of its use as a food was in France in 1623. The type we know was developed around 200 years ago.

Celery is a biennial. The first year only the plant we eat and are familiar with grows. The second year is when it blooms and sets its seed.

It was the custom to blanch the celery by piling dirt around it to make it white and to make the flavor mild. Newer, more gently flavored varieties make this practice no longer necessary.

Celeriac, also called nob celery or turnip-rooted celery, is a separate variety grown for its large, edible root. If you have ever eaten a bit of the tender inside root or core of celery you already know what celeriac tastes like.

CELERIAC

Selection

Choose firm, clean roots. Look for the smoother ones with fewer indentations and with fewer extra side roots. Remember, there will be a 10 to 15 percent loss in paring the vegetable.

Preparation

Wash the celeriac root and then pare it deep enough to get off the skin and most of the dark spots. This may be as deep as 1/4 inch. With the tip of the knife, remove the remaining dark spots where the side roots were attached.

Celeriac is usually sliced or diced before cooking although it can be cooked whole. When dicing, try to cut it into uniform-sized pieces to allow for even cooking. In slicing, cut the end slices a little thicker than the middle ones so that each slice will be nearly the same in the amount of celeriac.

Cooking

Fresh

Celeriac usually is found fresh only. For a 1 1/2 to 2 1/2 pound (purchased weight) root, put the prepared root and 1/4 cup water in a covered casserole. Cook in the microwave oven, stirring several times, until tender (about 10 to 15 minutes). Allow 5 minutes standing time. The stirring is necessary for even cooking.

CELERY

Selection

Choose firm, solid celery with fleshy, succulent stalks. Celery that is pithy, woody, limp, or that has yellowed outer leaves should be avoided.

Preparation

138 Separate the stalks and wash thoroughly, especially if the celery is quite dirty. In some rare cases, the celery may need to be scrubbed with a vegetable brush. If the outer stalks are heavy and have very heavy, coarse strings, it may be desirable to cut off the outer layer with a paring knife or potato peeler.

Cooking

Celery is usually found fresh only. If whole stalks are to be cooked, use a rectangular cooking container such as a loaf dish. Lay half the stalks of celery with the heavy ends of the stalks to one end of the dish. Lay the other half of the stalks with their heavy end to the opposite end of the dish. Add 1/4 cup water. Cover with plastic wrap or wax paper and cook in the microwave oven until tender (about 10 to 12 minutes). It is very important to rearrange the stalks about halfway through the cooking process. Mentally divide the dish into quarters. At each end of the dish turn each of the two quarters over so that the stalks that were in the center of the dish are now on the outside.

If celery is to be diced or sliced, put 3 cups of the celery in a casserole with 1/4 cup water. Cook, covered, in the microwave oven, stirring twice, until the celery is tender (about 10 minutes).

Seasonings:	dill, garlic, lemon, mustard, onion, paprika, parsley, poppy seed, sesame seed, thyme, butter, salt, pepper
Sauces:	Allemande, Bearnaise, Béchamel, Cheese, Mornay, Parsley, Tomato, Velouté, and White sauces; French dressing; sour cream
Cheeses:	American, Blue, Cheddar, Cream, Gorgonzola, Gruyère, Monterey Jack, Parmesan, Romano, Stilton, Swiss
Wines:	chablis, rhine wine, sauterne
Nuts:	almonds, pumpkin seed, sunflower seed
Extra serving suggestions:	hot, in Béchamel sauce with poppy seed added
	hot, with sour cream and dill
	hot, with butter, lemon juice, dill, salt, and pepper
	cold, marinated in French dressing

CREAMED CELERY WITH BASIL

The touch of onion and basil add spark to the flavor of the creamed celery. Too often celery is relegated to playing a supporting role to other vegetables. Here it is the star.

Makes 4 servings
1/4 cup chopped onion
2 tablespoons butter
3 cups diced celery
1/4 teaspoon basil leaves, crushed

Preparation time 21 Min.
1 cup White sauce (refer to Sauces chapter)

Put the onion and butter in a covered casserole. Cook for 3 minutes in the microwave oven. Add the celery and basil. Cook, stirring twice, in the microwave oven until tender (about 10 minutes). Set aside.

Make 1 cup White sauce. Stir it into the celery. Reheat for 1 minute. Serve.

140 **Tip:** the liquid from the celery may be used as part of the liquid in the White sauce. If it is left on the celery, it will dilute the sauce and make it a bit thinner.

My Time Is _____ Min.

CELESTIAL CELERY

The flavor is slightly oriental for some reason. Celery is a rarely used vegetable, mainly for lack of good recipes for preparing it. Use this one often.

Makes 4 servings

3 slices bacon
1/2 cup chopped onion
3 cups celery, sliced into
1/4-inch thick
1/4 cup chopped parsley
2 tablespoons dry white wine

Preparation time 15 Min.

2 tablespoons beef broth
Salt and pepper to taste
1/2 teaspoon cornstarch
2 tablespoons beef stock

Put the bacon and onion in a small, covered casserole or dish and cook in the microwave oven 4 minutes, stirring after 2 minutes. Drain off and discard the excess bacon fat.

Put the celery, bacon-onion mixture, and all the remaining ingredients in a larger, covered casserole. Cook in the microwave oven until tender (about 10 minutes). Stir several times during the cooking period.

141

Tip: if beef stock is not available, stir 1/4 teaspoon concentrated beef bouillon into 1/4 cup hot water to dissolve. Try substituting chicken broth for the beef broth for a flavor change.

My Time Is _____ Min.

AMERICAN CELERIAC SALAD

What a nice change this will be from potato salad. Make it for your next pot luck dinner or picnic. Make it often for your family. This one is really tasty.

Makes 4 servings

Preparation time 20 Min.

- 2 pounds celeriac (celery root)
- 1 clove garlic, finely minced
- 1/4 cup water
- 1/4 cup diced onion
- 1/4 cup diced sweet pickle
- 3 hard-boiled eggs, peeled and diced (cooked conventionally)
- 1/2 cup mayonnaise
- 2 tablespoons lemon juice
- 1 teaspoon dill weed
- 1/4 teaspoon salt
  Pepper to taste

Peel the celeriac and cut into 1/2-inch cubes. Put the celeriac, garlic, and water in a covered casserole and cook in the microwave oven, stirring occasionally, until tender. (This should take about 12 minutes.) Chill.

142 Add the onion, sweet pickle, and eggs. Mix together the mayonnaise, lemon juice, dill weed, salt, and pepper. Gently stir into the celeriac.

Tip: try to get the cubes of celeriac as uniform as possible for even cooking. Stirring is also necessary for even cooking. For a change of pace, substitute lime juice for the lemon juice.

My Time Is _____ Min.

HERBED CELERIAC
(CELERY ROOT) SALAD

If you like potato salad, the chances are very good that you will like celery root salad. It is not as starchy as potato salad. Use this when you want a cooked salad.

Makes 4 servings   *Preparation time 20 Min.*

2 pounds celeriac (celery root)	2 teaspoons sugar
1/4 cup water	1/4 teaspoon pepper
1 teaspoon lemon juice	1 1/4 teaspoons dry mustard
6 tablespoons olive oil or salad oil	1 clove garlic, minced
3 tablespoons white wine vinegar (or 2 1/2 tablespoons distilled white vinegar)	1/3 cup sliced green onions
	1/3 cup snipped parsley
	3/4 teaspoon dill weed
	1 hard-boiled egg, sliced (cooked conventionally)
1 teaspoon salt	1/4 cup sliced ripe olives

Rinse, scrub, and peel the celery root. Cut into 1/2-inch cubes. Put the celery root, water, and lemon juice in a covered casserole and cook in the microwave oven until tender (about 10 to 12 minutes). Drain. Combine the remaining ingredients and pour over the celery root. Chill and marinate at least 2 hours. Serve on lettuce leaves. Garnish with sliced hard-boiled egg and sliced ripe olives.

143

Tip: the lemon juice is to help keep the celeriac white. The distilled vinegar is stronger flavored and higher in acetic acid than the wine vinegar. White vinegar is used to keep the salad whiter. Do not try to cook an egg in the shell in the microwave oven. If you are lucky, the egg explodes while it is still in the oven. Think that one through.

My Time Is _____ *Min.*

CORN

Originally the term corn was used to refer to the leading grain crop of a district, thus in England it meant wheat, and in Scotland and Ireland it meant oats. Maize, the principal cereal of the New World, was first known as "Indian Corn" and then, later, as corn.

Corn is a member of the grass family and was brought to Europe after 1492. Evidence of corn being grown in Mexico dates back 80,000 years. Corn was found growing from Chile to Canada wherever fields were cultivated. Within 50 years of the discovery of the New World corn was being grown in Europe, Africa, India, Tibet, and China.

It is the green corn or the immature corn that we eat as a vegetable. Matured corn is ground into corn meal. Mature corn kernels soaked in lye water give us hominy.

Selection

Corn-on-the-cob is the only way fresh corn is usually available. First of all, try to select all the ears of the same size to allow even cooking. Try to select ears with full rows of kernels that are plump and firm. In general, the bigger and more yellow the kernels, the more mature the corn and the higher the starch content. Light yellow coloring and smaller kernels are indications of a sweeter, younger ear. Although corn will keep for several days without spoiling in your refrigerator, it will taste sweeter and better if used as soon as possible.

Preparation

You have a choice of two preparation methods for corn-on-the-cob. The first is for cooking the corn in the husks. Pull the husks back carefully so as to expose the silk. Remove all the silk. Pull the husks back into place and secure with a rubber band or two. The rubber will not heat in the microwave oven so will have no odor.

The second method is to remove all husks and silk. The ears may be individually wrapped in wax paper or plastic wrap.

In either method of preparation, cut out any bad spots. If the ear is not full to the tip, break off the tip.

If you wish to cut the corn off the cob, first remove any bad spots. Use a sharp knife such as a carving knife. Place the butt end of the corn securely on a cutting board. Starting at the tip, cut downward as deeply as possible to remove all of the kernels without cutting into the cob. Continue cutting around the ear until all kernels are off. Discard the cob.

Cooking

Fresh

For corn-on-the-cob, if only 1 ear is to be cooked, put it in the oven. It will need about 3 minutes to cook.

If 2 ears are being cooked, place them apart in the oven. They will need about 4 to 6 minutes cooking time.

If 3 or more ears are to be cooked, place them in a wheel-spoke pattern with the tip of the ears at the hub and the base to the outside. Four ears take 7 to 10 minutes, while 6 ears take 9 to 12 minutes. Turn the ears over halfway through the cooking period.

For cut corn, put the corn in a covered casserole. Usually no water need be added as there should be enough "milk" from the corn to help cook it. Cooking time will depend upon the amount of corn. The corn from 4 ears should take about 5 minutes cooking time, while that from 6 ears will take about 7 minutes. Stir the corn twice during the cooking period.

Frozen

For corn-on-the-cob, wrap the individual ears in wax paper or plastic wrap. If one ear only is to be cooked, put it in the oven and cook until done and tender, about 4 to 6 minutes. If 2 ears are being cooked, place them apart in the oven and cook from 6 to 8 minutes.

If 3 or more ears are to be cooked, place them in a wheel-spoke pattern with the tips of the ears at the hub and the base ends to the outside. Four ears take 10 to 12 minutes, while 6 ears take from 12 to 16 minutes. Turn the ears over halfway through the cooking period.

Sometimes the corn needs reheating after standing a short time. This is because the cool corn cob steals heat from the kernels.

For cut corn, put the corn and 2 tablespoons water in a covered casserole. Cook in the microwave oven, stirring twice during the cooking period, until as done as you like. A 10-ounce package will take 5 to 7 minutes.

Canned

Canned corn is fully cooked and only needs reheating before being used.

Seasonings:	cayenne, chili powder, onion, parsley, butter, salt, pepper, sugar
Sauce:	Tomato
Cheeses:	American, Cheddar, Monterey Jack, Parmesan, Romano, Swiss
Nuts	pine nuts, sunflower seed
Extra serving suggestions:	hot, with butter, salt, and a dash of cayenne
	hot, cooked with onion and red and green peppers

147

CORN-FETTI

From Mexico comes a dish known as Colachi. Here is a delightful take-off that is not only delicious but fun to eat. The title comes from the pieces of brightly colored vegetables.

Makes 4 servings

- 1 cup water in 2-cup measure
- 1/4 cup chopped celery
- 1/4 cup chopped onion
- 1/4 teaspoon chili powder (optional)
- 2 tablespoons butter
- 1 medium green pepper (cut into strips)

Preparation time 20 Min.

- 2 medium ears of corn (cut into 1-inch pieces)
- 2 medium tomatoes (peeled, cored, and cut into eighths)
- Salt to taste

148 Heat the water to a boil in the microwave oven. Use it to dip the tomatoes into before peeling so that they will peel easily. Put the celery, onion, chili powder, and butter in a covered casserole. Cook in the microwave oven for 4 minutes. Stir in the green pepper strips. Cook, covered, for 2 minutes. Stir in the corn pieces. Cook, covered, for 4 minutes. Stir in the tomatoes and salt. Cook, covered, for 2 minutes. Serve.

Tip: serve one little corn holder with each dish. The pieces of corn are too hot to hold in one's fingers. The corn holder is stuck into the corn so that the kernels may be nibbled off.

My Time Is _____ Min.

EGGPLANT

Like the tomato and the avocado, the eggplant is a fruit that is used as a vegetable. This plant is a member of the nightshade family. It is a native of Southern and Eastern Asia. It is a very important food in all the areas surrounding the Mediterranean Sea and in the Orient.

The variety usually used is a dark, shiny purple but there are also white, red, yellow, and striped ones. This fruit requires warm weather for growing.

Selection

There are two general types of eggplant available. The first, the large purple one so popular throughout the Mediterranean areas, is the one usually seen. The other is the small Oriental eggplant about twice the size of an egg. Either may be used in recipes but when a recipe calls for 1 eggplant, then use about 1 to 1 1/2 pounds of the oriental eggplant.

Look for fruit with a bright, shiny, dark purple coloring. Check for bruises and brown spots. Under-ripe eggplant may be bitter and will not have a well-developed flavor. Eggplant that has been held too long will have shriveled and become soft.

Preparation

Rinse the eggplant. Then prepare it any way you choose, halved, quartered, in wedges, sliced, or diced. The important thing is to have each piece, sliced or what have you, be the same size as all the others to allow for even cooking in the microwave oven.

When possible, sprinkle all cut areas with salt and let stand on toweling, paper or cloth, to soak up the moisture. The salt pulls out any bitter juices. Rinse off the salt and pat dry before using. On rare occasions there is an eggplant that nothing helps. If you find such a bitter one, discard it. Unfortunately, such a discovery usually occurs after the eggplant is cooked and served.

Whether to peel or not depends on how the eggplant is used. Eggplant gets quite soft when cooked and the skin will help hold it together. On the other hand, the skin remains tough after cooking.

The skin is so thin that the meat of the eggplant can be removed from it easily during the eating process. Always pare, if the eggplant is to be sliced or diced.

Cooking

Fresh

As eggplant comes fresh only, no other cooking instructions are given.

Generally, if the eggplant is cooked in halves, quarters, or wedges, the skin is left on. Put the eggplant and 2 tablespoons water in a covered casserole. If a large enough casserole is not available, use a rectangular baking dish and cover with wax paper or plastic wrap.

If two halves are being cooked, set them as far apart as possible in the dish. If quarters or wedges are being cooked, try to arrange them wheel-spoke fashion, if possible. If not, the pieces will need rearranging during the cooking process to obtain even cooking.

150 If the eggplant is sliced, try to place it in a single layer in a round or rectangular dish. Smaller pieces should be placed in the center and larger pieces on the outer edge. If the slices must be piled on top of each other, they will have to be rearranged during the cooking period to obtain even cooking. As slices become tender, move them to the middle of the dish. Move less tender pieces to the outer edge.

If the vegetable is diced, any covered casserole will suffice. As above, add 2 tablespoons water. Stirring is a must and should be done at least twice during the cooking period for even cooking.

An eggplant normally takes 5 to 9 minutes to cook depending on its size and maturity. The addition of a sauce or other materials will affect the cooking time, too. For some reason, different pieces of the same fruit cook at different rates of speed. Always remove any more tender pieces before they overcook.

Seasonings:	basil, celery seed, chili powder, cinnamon, clove, garlic, lemon, marjoram, mint, onion, oregano, paprika, parsley, poppy seed, sage, sesame seed, butter, salt, pepper
Sauces:	Allemande, Garlic, Hot Poppy Seed, and Tomato sauces; French dressing; sour cream; yogurt
Cheeses:	Monterey Jack, Mozzarella, Parmesan, Provolone, Ricotta, Romano, Swiss
Wines:	chablis, rhine wine, rosé, sauterne, sherry, dry vermouth
Nuts:	almonds, pine nuts, pistachios, pumpkin seed, sunflower seed
Extra serving suggestions:	hot, cooked with currents, pine nuts, onions, and cinnamon
	hot, with butter, Parmesan cheese, salt, and pepper
	hot, with butter, chopped mint, chopped parsley, salt, and pepper
	hot, with butter, lemon, sesame seed, salt, and pepper

BAKED EGGPLANT WITH CHEESE AND TOMATOES

Eggplant is one of the most widely used vegetables in the world. Here is a French version that is certain to be a hit with your family.

Makes 6 to 8 servings

- 1 cup minced onions
- 2 tablespoons olive or salad oil
- 1 can (1 pound) tomatoes
- 1 bay leaf
- 1/4 teaspoon thyme
  Pinch of saffron
- 1 large clove garlic, minced

Preparation time 40 Min.

- 1/4 teaspoon salt
- 2 pounds eggplant
  salt
- 2 ounces Swiss cheese, sliced into 1/16-inch-thick pieces
  Olive or salad oil

Cook the onions, covered, in the oil for 4 minutes in the microwave oven. Drain the tomatoes and reserve the juice. Rub tomatoes through a sieve to remove the seeds. Add tomatoes, bay leaf, thyme, saffron, garlic, and 1/4 teaspoon salt to the onion. Cook, uncovered, until thick enough to hold shape softly in a spoon.

152

Peel and cut the eggplant into 1/2-inch slices. Sprinkle with salt and let set on paper toweling for 20 minutes to pull out any bitter juices. Rinse, pat dry, and brush with oil. The eggplant may be sautéed lightly to brown, if desired, but this is optional. Place one layer of eggplant in a 2-quart rectangular (12″ × 9″) baking dish. Spread with half of the tomato sauce, then a row of half of the cheese. Add the remaining eggplant, cover with the remaining tomato sauce and then the remaining cheese. Add 1/4 to 1/2 cup of the tomato juice. Cover and cook in the microwave oven until tender. This should take about 10 to 15 minutes. Remove cover if too much liquid builds up.

Tip: this is best if made with Italian-style pear tomatoes, but regular tomatoes can be substituted. Oregano may be substituted for the thyme.

My Time Is _____ Min.

EGGPLANT WITH DRIED-FRUIT STUFFING

From the Somali-Ethiopian area comes this different and intriguing recipe. The stuffing tastes equally fine in a duck. Be adventurous and try this unusual dish.

Makes 4 servings *Preparation time 30 Min.*

3 tablespoons oil or butter	1/3 cup chopped dates
1 clove garlic, minced	1/3 cup chopped walnuts
1 medium-sized onion, chopped	1/2 cup white wine
	1/2 teaspoon salt
1 medium-sized green pepper, chopped	1/2 teaspoon cinnamon
	1/2 teaspoon clove
1 cup mixed dried fruits, chopped (prunes, apricots)	1/2 teaspoon paprika
	1 1/2 cups cooked rice
	2 eggplants (or 1 duck)

Put the oil, garlic, onion, and pepper in a small, covered casserole. Cook in the microwave oven until tender (about 6 minutes). Add the fruits, dates, walnuts, wine, and seasonings. Mix well and cook, covered, 4 minutes more. Stir in the rice. Put in the microwave oven long enough to heat the rice through. Meanwhile, cut the eggplants in half and scoop out the center, leaving a 3/4-inch wall. Fill with the rice-fruit mixture. Cook, covered, in the microwave oven in a rectangular baking dish (12″ × 9″) until the eggplant is tender (about 10 to 15 minutes more).

153

If cooking a duck, stuff with rice-fruit mixture, tie legs together, and fold the wings under the body. Cook breast-side down for 20 minutes. Drain. Cook breast-side up another 20 minutes or until duck is tender.

Tip: this eggplant dish is also good chilled.

My Time Is _____ *Min.*

EGGPLANT SALAD

In the countries of the Eastern Mediterranean region, many foods served cold as salads are different from our ideas of what a salad should be. Try this one from Greece. It could be the feature dish at a luncheon.

Makes 6 servings

- 2 eggplants
- 2 tablespoons lemon juice
- 2 tablespoons minced onion
- 2 tomatoes, peeled and chopped
- 1 clove garlic, minced

Preparation time 20 Min.

- 1/2 teaspoon oregano
- 1 tablespoon wine vinegar
- 3 tablespoons olive or salad oil
- 1/2 teaspoon salt
- Pepper to taste

Cut the eggplants in half and cook in a covered casserole in the microwave oven until fork-tender (about 10 to 15 minutes). Rearrange while cooking, if they are not cooking evenly. Chill. Peel. Discard the centers if too seedy (if not, use them). Dice the eggplant into small pieces. Add the remaining ingredients and mix carefully so as not to mash the eggplant. Chill well before serving. May be served on a bed of lettuce.

154

Tip: put the thicker parts of the eggplant to the outside of the casserole while cooking. This will help the eggplant cook more evenly. Sometimes, rearrangement will also be needed. Do not overcook the vegetable as that will leave it mushy.

My Time Is _____ Min.

EGGPLANT SHAHARAZAD

Eggplant, one of the most popular vegetables around the world, and yet one used too seldom in our own diets, is the basis of this dish. It will serve as both vegetable and starch dish.

Makes 4 servings

- 1 medium-large eggplant
  Salt
- 2 tablespoons butter
- 2 tablespoons chopped onion
- 2 tablespoons chopped parsley
- 1 teaspoon crumbled dried mint leaves
- 1/4 teaspoon salt

Preparation time 45 Min.

Pepper to taste
- 3 tablespoons currants or chopped raisins
- 3 tablespoons chopped pine nuts or walnuts
- 2 tablespoons tomato purée
- 1/4 teaspoon cinnamon
- 1 teaspoon sugar
- 2 cups hot cooked rice

Peel and slice the eggplant into 1/2-inch slices. Sprinkle with salt and let set on paper toweling for 20 minutes to draw out the bitter juices. Rinse and pat dry. Cut into 1″ × 1″ × 1/2″ pieces. Cook, covered, in a casserole in the microwave oven, stirring several times, until tender. (This should take about 10 to 12 minutes.) Set aside. Put the butter, onion, parsley, and mint leaves in a large, covered casserole. Cook, covered, in the microwave oven, stirring at least once, for 4 minutes. Stir in the 1/4 teaspoon salt, pepper, currants, pine nuts, tomato purée, cinnamon, and sugar. Cook, covered, 3 minutes more. Stir in the rice. Cook, covered, 3 minutes more. Very gently stir in the eggplant. Cook, covered, 2 to 3 minutes more to reheat through.

155

Tip: be prepared to get hooked on this way of fixing eggplant. As always, allow a little time for the residual cooking in judging the doneness of the eggplant.

My Time Is _____ Min.

STUFFED EGGPLANT

Iran sends us a stuffed eggplant dish quite different from those found in our own country. Serve as a vegetable dish with roast lamb. Somehow, our neighbors found the affinity that eggplant and lamb have for each other. Try this and see for yourself.

Makes 4 servings   *Preparation time 25 Min.*

2 small eggplants	1 bay leaf
1 cup chopped onion	1 stick cinnamon
2 cloves garlic, minced	1/2 teaspoon salt
2 tablespoons olive or salad oil	Dash of pepper
2 cups chopped tomato	8 black olives (optional)
1/4 cup chopped parsley	4 rolled anchovy fillets (optional)

Cut the eggplants in half. Scoop out the centers, leaving a wall of flesh 3/4-inch thick. Chop the eggplant that was scooped out. Cook the onion and garlic in the oil in a covered 1-quart casserole for 4 minutes. Add the tomato, parsley, chopped eggplant, bay leaf, cinnamon stick, salt, and pepper. Cook, covered, 5 minutes, stirring once.

156

Remove the bay leaf and cinnamon stick and divide the contents of the casserole among the four eggplant halves. Put in a rectangular baking dish with the larger ends of the eggplant toward the ends of the dish. Cover with wax paper or plastic wrap and cook in the microwave oven until tender (about 10 minutes). Garnish with the olives and the anchovy fillets.

Tip: putting the thicker ends of the eggplant toward the ends of the cooking dish ensures more even cooking of irregularly shaped pieces of food.

My Time Is _____ Min.

EGGPLANT AND YOGURT SALAD

From Iran, here is a salad of eggplant and yogurt. Yogurt is used in many ways and in many dishes throughout the Near East. This salad is a bit like the *Eggplant Salad* recipe in that the salad is made of cooked, chilled eggplant. It is a bit like the *Beet and Yogurt Salad* in that yogurt is used in the dressing, but it has a taste and verve all its own.

Makes 6 servings   *Preparation time 20 Min.*

2 eggplants	2 cups (1 pint) yogurt
1 clove garlic, minced	1/2 teaspoon salt
1 cup peeled, chopped	1/8 teaspoon pepper
tomato	2 tablespoons
1 tablespoon olive or salad	finely-chopped walnuts
oil	1 teaspoon dill weed

Cut the eggplants in half and cook in a covered casserole in the microwave oven until fork-tender (about 10 to 15 minutes). Rearrange while cooking if they are not cooking evenly. Chill. Peel. Discard the centers if they are too seedy (if not, use them). Dice the eggplant into small pieces.

157

Mix the garlic, 3/4 cup tomato, olive oil, yogurt, salt, and pepper. Add to the eggplant and mix carefully so as to not mash the eggplant. Garnish with 1/4 cup tomato, nuts, and dill weed. Serve chilled. May be served on a bed of lettuce.

Tip: put the thicker parts of the eggplant to the outer perimeter of the casserole while cooking. This will help the eggplant cook more evenly. Sometimes rearrangement will also be needed. Do not overcook the vegetable, as that will leave it mushy.

My Time Is _____ *Min.*

GREEN PEPPERS

All peppers are of the capsicum genus of the nightshade family and are related to the tomato. The pepper is the edible fruit of the plant. In the tropics it is a perennial plant, but in the temperate areas it is used as an annual as it frost-kills.

Peppers come in many sizes, shapes, colors, and degrees of hotness or mildness. For the purpose of this book, sweet green peppers will be the main consideration. Sweet red peppers are the same as the green ones, the difference being that they were left on the plant longer to mature a bit more and to turn red as they ripened.

In hotness peppers range from the sweet mildness of paprika and pimiento to the firey hotness of chile tepins and cayenne. In general, the larger peppers are the sweeter ones and the smaller peppers are the hotter ones. Most hot peppers are used as seasoning or are pickled.

Selection

Look for firm dark green peppers, without blemishes, that are well formed. Green peppers with red patches or all red peppers are the same as the green peppers except they have been allowed to mature longer. Avoid wilted or shriveled peppers as they have been held too long and have lost their freshness.

Preparation

Wash the peppers. If the peppers are to be used whole, cut through the pepper in a circle around the stem, almost to the bottom of the pepper. Gently pull the stem and core out. Cut out any whitish green rib material that remains inside the pepper. Cut out any blemishes. The pepper is now ready to cook.

If the pepper is to be cut up, cut through the pepper in a circle around the stem. Cut the pepper in half lengthwise, starting at the top of one side and going around to the top on the other side. Pull the pepper apart. Remove the core and cut out any whitish green rib material from the inside of the pepper. Cut out any blemishes. Cut the peppers into the desired pieces. They are now ready to cook.

Cooking

Fresh

As green peppers come fresh only, no other cooking instructions are given.

If the peppers are being cooked whole but not stuffed, put them in a covered casserole. Cook them in the microwave oven until they are tender, about 7 minutes for 1 pound of peppers. Halfway through the cooking period, turn each pepper over or halfway around, depending on how they are placed.

If the peppers are cut up, put them in a covered casserole. Cook them in the microwave oven until tender, about 7 minutes for 1 pound of peppers. Stir them once during the cooking period.

Seasonings:	basil, bay, cayenne, celery seed, chili powder, chives, cumin (comino), curry powder, garlic, ginger, lemon, marjoram, mint, mustard, onion, oregano, paprika, parsley, rosemary, savory, thyme, butter, salt, pepper, olive oil
Sauces:	Tomato; sour cream
Cheeses:	American, Cheddar, Gruyère, Monterey Jack, Mozzarella, Parmesan, Provolone, Ricotta, Romano, Swiss
Wines:	burgundy, chablis, rosé, sauterne, sherry
Nuts:	almonds, peanuts, pine nuts, pumpkin seed, sunflower seed
Extra serving suggestions:	hot, cooked with crumbled bacon and grated cheddar cheese
	cold, cooked and marinated in oil and vinegar or lemon juice with a touch of garlic

SAUTÉED GREEN PEPPERS

Here is a recipe from the Primavera family of Italy. The olive oil gives this dish its distinctive flavor.

Makes 4 servings	*Preparation time 15 Min.*
8 green peppers	1/4 teaspoon salt
1/4 cup olive oil	1/8 teaspoon pepper

Wash, core, and seed the peppers and cut them into strips. Put the peppers and oil into a covered casserole and cook in the microwave oven until the peppers are tender. (This will take about 7 to 8 minutes.) If too much liquid accumulates, cook with the cover off for the last minute or two. Add the seasonings.

Tip: olive oil has a distinctive flavor, but other oils can be substituted (with some loss of taste). Also, you can use butter or margarine, if you wish.

161

My Time Is _____ Min.

PEPPERS AND TOMATOES

Try this Austrian version of peppers and tomatoes, made rich
and succulent with the addition of a flavorful semi-soft cheese.

Makes 4 servings   *Preparation time 30 Min.*

1/2 pound bacon	1/4 teaspoon salt
2 onions cut into rings	1/8 teaspoon pepper
1 clove garlic, minced	1/4 teaspoon thyme
4 green peppers, seeded and cut into strips	1/2 cup dry white wine
1 pound tomatoes, peeled and cut into wedges	1 cup diced semi-soft cheese (Gruyère or Port du Salut)

Cook the bacon until crisp on a microwave oven roasting rack or
on overturned saucers in a large rectangular dish (about 10 minutes). Crumble the bacon. Reserve 2 tablespoons bacon drippings. In a covered casserole, add the onion, garlic, and peppers
to the 2 tablespoons bacon drippings. Cook in the microwave
oven for 5 minutes. Add the tomatoes, seasonings, and wine. Stir.
Cook, covered, 5 minutes more. Add the cheese and crumbled
bacon. Reheat long enough to melt the cheese. Serve with dark
162 bread.

Tip: to peel the tomatoes easily, drop for a few moments into boiling hot water (to loosen the skins) and then into cold water (to
cool rapidly). The skins will slip off easily.

My Time Is _____ Min.

GREENS

There is no single history for greens. Greens include all of the lettuces, watercress, chard, spinach, dandelions, and some of the cabbages. Greens include most plants where the tender green leafy parts are eaten.

Many greens are biennials, that is the green leafy parts form the first year, while the plant flowers and sets its seed the second year. Also, most greens are cool weather crops.

Beet greens and chard come from the beet family. Kale and collards are a form of cabbage. Mustard greens originated in India. As its name indicates, it is the plant we get mustard seeds from. Turnip greens may be from a special variety although the tops of any young turnip may be eaten. Dandelions are a member of the chicory family and are very strongly flavored. The name comes from the French, *dent de lion,* which means tooth of the lion— which refers to the deeply indented leaves. Commercial dandelions are a special variety but those growing in your lawn are equally edible if young enough.

The secret is to pick greens when they are young and tender, cook them in their own steam, and do not overcook them. Then you will have the best of both flavor and texture.

163

Selection

Included under greens are spinach, chard, mustard, kale, collards, beet tops, turnip tops, and dandelions. This is not a complete list of greens but it is sufficient to get you started.

No matter what variety of green leafy plant you are looking for, the same general rules apply. Look for bright color, crispness, lack of blemishes, and tender young leaves. As the plants mature, the leaves get coarser, more leathery, and often the flavor becomes stronger and less pleasant.

Preparation

Wash, wash, wash, especially if the leaves are quite dirty. If there is a chance of little house guests in the leaves, soak a few minutes in salt water. After the leaves are clean, drain. Enough water will cling to the leaves to cook them with.

Cooking

Fresh

Whether to leave on the stems or not is a matter of personal preference. For chard, and any other leafy stemmed greens, it is best to cut the stem and the larger part of the veining (white or red, depending on the variety) from the leaf. This should be cut into bite-sized pieces and partly cooked before adding the green part of the leaves.

Whether to cook the leaves whole or cut up is a matter of personal preference.

Cook all greens in a covered casserole. Stir during the cooking period. Greens with thinner, more tender leaves, such as spinach, need only be cooked until they are wilted and hot. Greens with thicker, more leathery leaves, such as chard or kale, need to be cooked longer. Cooking times are not given, as the amount, the age, and the variety affect the cooking times. Most greens will cook tender in just a few minutes.

Frozen

164 Put the frozen greens in a covered casserole, icy-side up, and cook, stirring at least one time, until they are hot and tender. A 10-ounce package of spinach, the leaf green that is most often frozen, cooks in about 6 to 7 minutes.

Canned

Canned greens are fully cooked. They need only to be heated before using.

Seasonings:	basil, fennel, lemon, marjoram, mint, mustard, onion, oregano, poppy seed, rosemary, sesame seed, tarragon, thyme, butter, salt, pepper, vinegar
Sauces:	Allemande, Bearnaise, Butter and Seed, Cheese, Garlic, Hollandaise, Hot Poppy Seed, Mornay, and Tomato; sour cream; yogurt; French dressing; vinegar and oil dressing
Cheeses:	American, Blue, Cheddar, Farmer, Gorgonzola, Gruyère, Monterey Jack, Mozzarella, Parmesan, Provolone, Romano, Rouquefort, Stilton, Swiss

Wines:	chablis, rhine wine, rosé, sauterne, sherry, dry vermouth
Nuts:	almonds, brazil nuts, peanuts, pine nuts, pumpkin seed, sunflower seed, walnuts, water chestnuts
Extra serving suggestions:	this is too broad a field for specific suggestions

165

CREAMY COLLARDS

Collards are a member of the cabbage family. Unlike most "greens" they need to be cooked a fairly long time. Being a member of the cabbage family, they should be cooked until tender, but overcooking will cause them to develop a strong, unpleasant taste.

Makes 4 servings		*Preparation time 20 Min.*
1/4	cup chopped onion	2 tablespoons flour
2	tablespoons butter or	1/4 cup water
	margarine	1 bunch collards
1/4	teaspoon celery seed	1 cup milk
1/4	teaspoon curry powder	Salt to taste

Put the onion, butter, celery seed, and curry powder in a covered casserole and cook 3 minutes. Wash and drain the collards. Cut off any coarse stems. Cut the leaves into large bite-sized pieces.

Stir the flour into the onion mixture. Blend in the water. Add the collards and stir to coat with the sauce. Cook, covered, in the microwave oven, stirring several times, until tender (about 10 to 12 **166** minutes).

Blend in the milk and salt. Cook, covered, until hot. Serve.

Tip: a very good addition to this recipe would be several strips of crumbled, crisply cooked bacon.

My Time Is _____ Min.

MUSTARD GREENS

An update on the old, old way of preparing "greens." Now we cook them in the microwave oven and we studiously avoid overcooking them; no more cooking the life out of vegetables.

Makes 4 servings

Preparation time 10 Min.

- 4 strips bacon, diced
- 2 bunches mustard greens
- 2 tablespoons bacon drippings
- 1 teaspoon wine vinegar

Salt and pepper to taste

Cook the bacon in a casserole in the microwave oven until crisp, stirring once or twice to separate the bacon pieces. While the bacon is cooking, wash, drain, and coarsely chop the mustard leaves. With a slotted spoon, remove the bacon. Discard all but 2 tablespoons of the bacon drippings. Put the mustard leaves in a large, covered casserole. Sprinkle on the bacon, bacon drippings, and vinegar. Cook, covered, in the microwave oven for 3 minutes. Stir, cover, and cook until tender, about 2 minutes more. Add the salt and pepper and gently stir. Serve.

Tip: all "greens" should be cooked soft and tender but never until they are mushy. Virtually every vegetable deserves to have some of its texture preserved. **167**

SPINACH WITH PIMIENTO

From Mexico comes a delightful way to fix spinach that will please the palate and the wallet. Spinach is a good source of vitamin A, calcium, and potassium. Many people dislike spinach only because they have tasted it overcooked by the conventional method. But in the microwave oven, cooked only until it is wilted, it is another story.

Makes 4 to 6 servings   *Preparation time 15 Min.*

2 pounds fresh spinach	1/3 cup milk
2 tablespoons olive oil	2 hard-boiled eggs, sliced
1 clove garlic, finely minced	(cooked conventionally)
1 tablespoon butter or	3 large, canned pimientos,
margarine	cut into small strips
1 tablespoon flour	

168 Wash the spinach thoroughly and drain well. Cut into large bite-sized pieces. Put the olive oil and garlic in a large, covered casserole. Cook in the microwave oven for 3 minutes, stirring once. Stir in the spinach, cover, and cook in the microwave oven for 3 or 4 minutes, stirring once, or until the spinach has wilted. Set aside. Melt the butter in a 1-cup measure or small casserole in the microwave oven (about 30 seconds). Stir in the flour and then blend in the milk. Cook in the microwave oven, stirring once or twice, until the sauce is very thick. Continue cooking for 2 or 3 minutes more on defrost or low power. If these powers are not available, let the sauce sit for 2 minutes and then cook 1 minute more on high. Stir into the spinach until the spinach is well coated. Reheat a minute or two until the spinach is heated through. Garnish with the pimiento and the egg slices.

Tip: never cook an egg in the shell in the microwave oven. If you are lucky it will explode while it is still in the oven.

My Time Is _____ *Min.*

SPINACH AND RICE CASSEROLE

Here is a very unusual combination of a succulent vegetable and rice. It is quite good. It makes a nice side dish with any meat.

Makes 6 servings
1/3 cup olive oil
  2 pounds fresh spinach
1/2 cup chopped onion
  1 tablespoon chopped
        parsley

Preparation time 25 Min.
Salt and pepper to taste
1 cup raw rice
1 tablespoon tomato paste
    Water (1 1/2 to 2 cups)

Wash, drain, and coarsely chop the spinach. Put the olive oil, onion, parsley, spinach, salt, and pepper into a large casserole. Cook, covered, in the microwave oven 5 minutes. The spinach will cook down considerably.

Just before adding the rice, make a nest of the spinach by putting some of it up the sides of the casserole and some on the bottom. It makes for a prettier dish. Add the rice, tomato paste, and water. Cover the casserole and return to the microwave oven. Cook 15 minutes more, stirring carefully so as to not disturb the spinach nest. Let stand 5 minutes before serving.

169

Tip: add only the 1 1/2 cups water at first. If a lot of water has clung to the spinach, that is all that will be needed. If very little water clung to the spinach, the additional 1/2 cup can be added near the end of the cooking period if it is needed.

My Time Is _____ *Min.*

SPINACH AND NUT SALAD

In this salad of cooked spinach from Iran, the blend of spinach and yogurt is one you will surely relish. Expect curtain calls for this salad.

Makes 4 servings

1 1/2 pounds (2 bunches) fresh spinach
1/2 cup minced onion
1 tablespoon olive oil
1 cup yogurt
1 clove garlic, minced

Preparation time 15 Min.

1/2 teaspoon salt
1/8 teaspoon pepper
2 tablespoons chopped fresh mint or 1 teaspoon dried mint
1/2 cup chopped walnuts

Wash the spinach thoroughly and drain. Remove coarse stems and chop finely. Put in a covered casserole and cook in the microwave oven until barely tender (about 4 to 5 minutes). Add the onion and oil to the spinach and mix carefully so as not to mash the vegetable. Add the garlic, salt, pepper, and mint to the yogurt. Stir gently into the spinach. Chill. Garnish with the nuts.

170 **Tip:** take care not to overcook the spinach and to allow for residual cooking. The spinach should be tender but not mushy.

My Time Is _____ Min.

NORWEGIAN SPINACH SOUP

Spinach, being a cool-weather crop, grows well in the short Nordic summers, so it is often used. Try this soup as the first course of a dinner or the main course of a luncheon.

Makes 8 servings
- 2 packages frozen chopped spinach
- 6 cups beef bouillon or 6 teaspoons beef bouillon concentrate and 6 cups water
- 3 tablespoons butter or margarine

Preparation time 35 Min.
- 2 tablespoons flour
- Salt and pepper to taste
- 2 hard-boiled eggs, peeled and sliced (cooked conventionally)

Put the spinach in a covered casserole and cook in the microwave oven until tender (about 10 to 12 minutes), stirring several times. Drain and reserve all the liquid from the spinach. Use the liquid as part of the 6 cups bouillon. Keep the spinach as warm as possible.

Melt the butter and mix in the flour. Stir in the bouillon gradually. **171** Bring the bouillon to a boil, covered, stirring once or twice. Continue cooking for 2 or 3 minutes more on defrost or low power. If these powers are not available, let the sauce sit for 2 minutes and then cook 1 minute more on high. Add the spinach, salt, and pepper. Blend thoroughly. Bring to a simmer. Serve with the egg slices floating on top.

Tip: when cooking frozen spinach, no water is added. If fresh spinach is used, chop it fine. No water need be added here either, as spinach is a very succulent vegetable and has enough liquid in it to cook itself. Never cook an egg in the shell in the microwave oven as it may explode.

My Time Is _____ Min.

SWISS CHARD GRATINÉED

Choose tender, bright green chard for this recipe. The microwave oven will keep it bright green and delicious.

Makes 4 servings   *Preparation time 20 Min.*
2 bunches Swiss chard   1/4 cup heavy cream
1/4 cup flour   1/4 cup grated Parmesan
1/2 cup water   cheese
1 tablespoon lemon juice   1 tablespoon butter
1 egg yolk   Salt and pepper to taste

Wash and trim any blemishes from the chard. Cut the green part of each leaf from the white rib and stalk. Cut the white parts into 1/2-inch pieces. Blend the flour and water together to make a smooth paste. Add the lemon juice. Bring to a boil in a covered casserole in the microwave oven, stirring several times. Add more liquid if needed to keep the sauce from becoming too thick, but remember that some liquid will cook out of the chard. Add the white part of the chard and cook, covered, until almost tender (about 4 to 5 minutes), stirring once or twice.

172 Meanwhile, cut the green leaves into large bite-sized pieces. Add the greens to the stems, stir, cover, and continue cooking in the microwave oven until tender (usually 5 to 6 minutes). Blend the egg yolk and cream and stir gradually into the chard. Heat to thicken, but take care not to let the sauce boil, as the egg may curdle. Stir in the Parmesan cheese and butter. Salt and pepper to taste. Serve piping hot.

Tip: the age of the chard and, hence, its tenderness, has a great effect on the cooking time, so no precise cooking time may be given. Also, the size of the bunches of chard, which affects the total amount, can change the cooking time. Let the chard get tender but not mushy. Other greens may be substituted, such as spinach or mustard.

My Time Is _____ *Min.*

JERUSALEM ARTICHOKE

The Jerusalem artichoke, also called the sun choke, is a member of the sunflower family and is a native of North America. It is not an artichoke but was given the name due to the similarity in flavor with the true artichoke.

It was an important part of the diet of some American Indian tribes. It was reported being grown in the gardens of Indians of the northeast when the first colonists settled there.

The plant is frost-tender but grows from the tubers. Just a few plants will provide enough tubers, the part that is eaten, to supply the average family for a year. If this vegetable is hard to find in your area, plant and raise your own.

One of the great advantages of the Jerusalem artichoke is that it contains no starch. The carbohydrates (other than the 1 to 3 percent free sugar) are thought to be of no food value to humans. This would indicate that this is a good food for diabetics and for those following the Atkin's diet.

173

Selection

Look for Jerusalem artichokes that are as smooth as possible, and as free of knobs as possible, for easier paring and for less waste. Look for plump, firm tubers. Tubers that have shriveled are well past their prime and should be avoided. Also beware of those that are soft or have decayed spots.

Preparation

Cut off and reserve all the larger knobs on the Jerusalem artichoke tuber. Peel the tubers and the reserved knobs. Wash and drain. The vegetable is now ready to be sliced, diced, grated, or cooked whole.

Cooking

Fresh

The artichoke may be cooked whole, cut into pieces, diced, sliced, or grated. Add 1/4 cup water to 1 pound of the vegetable. Cook, covered, stirring several times, in the microwave oven.

When being cooked whole, it may be necessary to remove the smaller pieces as they get tender, to avoid overcooking them, before the larger pieces get done. One pound of Jerusalem artichokes cooks in approximately 7 minutes. Stirring is necessary for even cooking.

Frozen

It is doubtful that this vegetable is available frozen. If it is found, put the contents of a package and 1/4 cup water in a covered casserole. Cook in the microwave oven, stirring several times, until tender. The time is estimated at 6 to 8 minutes.

Canned

It is doubtful that this vegetable is available canned. If it is found, it would be a simple case of reheating.

Seasonings:	basil, coriander, curry powder, dill, garlic, lemon, lime, onion, parsley, poppy seed, sesame seed, tarragon, thyme, butter, salt, pepper
Sauces:	Bearnaise, Hollandaise, Mornay, Tomato, and White sauces; mayonnaise; sour cream
Cheeses:	Parmesan, Romano
Extra serving suggestions:	cold, served with mayonnaise mixed with lemon juice and dill weed
	hot, served mashed with butter, salt, pepper, and onion

JERUSALEM ARTICHOKES EN CASSEROLE

Jerusalem artichokes are slightly sweet in flavor. Although they have no starch of their own, they can substitute in general for a potato casserole.

Makes 4 servings

1 1/2 pounds Jerusalem artichokes, peeled and coarsely grated
1/4 cup water
2 tablespoons butter
1 clove garlic, minced
1/4 cup onion, finely chopped
2 tablespoons flour
1 teaspoon chicken bouillon concentrate

Preparation time 25 Min.

1 cup milk
1 tablespoon dry white wine
1/2 teaspoon chili powder
1/4 teaspoon salt
Pepper to taste
1 egg yolk, beaten

Cook the grated Jerusalem artichokes with the water in a covered casserole, stirring several times, in the microwave oven until tender (about 8 minutes). Set aside. Put the butter, garlic, and onion in a 1-quart covered casserole and cook, covered, 3 minutes. Stir in the flour and chicken bouillon concentrate. Blend in the milk. Add the wine, chili powder, salt, and pepper. Cook, covered, stirring several times, until the sauce comes to a boil and thickens. Continue cooking for 2 or 3 minutes more on defrost or low power. If these powers are not available, let the sauce sit for 2 minutes and then cook 1 minute more on high. Work a little of the hot sauce gradually into the egg yolk. Mix the egg yolk into the remaining hot sauce. Stir in the Jerusalem artichokes. Put in a 1-quart ring mold and bake until the mixture is hot and sets (about 4 minutes). Let stand 5 minutes, then serve.

175

Tip: if you do not have a microwave-oven-proof ring mold, use a 1-quart casserole and put a small glass in the middle. Carefully spoon in the mixture. A ring mold is preferable for this dish to allow more even cooking, as the food is very dense.

My Time Is _____ Min.

JERUSALEM ARTICHOKES MANHATTAN

This recipe gives a hearty, robust flavor to Jerusalem artichokes. It is particularly good when the weather is nippy or when one has been working very hard. You will find it most satisfying.

Makes 6 servings

1	pound Jerusalem artichokes
1/4	cup water
2	tablespoons butter or margarine
1/4	cup celery, diced

Preparation time 20 Min.

1/4	cup onion, diced
1/2	cup tomato sauce
1	tablespoon lemon juice
	Salt and pepper to taste
	Water

Peel and dice the Jerusalem artichokes into 1/2-inch cubes. Put the vegetable and the water in a covered casserole in the microwave oven and cook, stirring several times, until tender. (This should take about 7 minutes.) Set aside.

176 Put the butter, celery, and onion in a small, covered dish and cook 3 minutes, stirring once, or until tender. Add to the Jerusalem artichokes, along with the tomato sauce, lemon juice, salt, and pepper. Add enough water to make a good sauce consistency, about 1/4 cup, and cook 3 minutes more to blend the flavors.

Tip: if your taste runs to really robust flavors, try adding 2 tablespoons of dry red wine in with the tomato sauce and a clove of finely-minced garlic in with the onion and celery.

My Time Is _____ Min.

PARSLIED JERUSALEM ARTICHOKES

Jerusalem artichokes are such a delightful vegetable and this is a simple, tasty way to prepare them. Because they are so easy to fix this way, the recipe will become one of your favorites.

Makes 4 servings   Preparation time 15 Min.
1   pound Jerusalem   1   tablespoon butter
    artichokes   1/4 cup chopped parsley
1/4 cup water   Salt and pepper to taste
1   teaspoon lemon juice

Peel, wash, and dice the Jerusalem artichokes into 1/2-inch pieces. Put the vegetable, water, and lemon juice into a covered casserole and cook, stirring 2 or 3 times, in the microwave oven until tender. (This should take about 7 minutes.)

Drain all the liquid from the Jerusalem artichokes into a small dish or casserole. Add the butter to the liquid. Cook, uncovered, in the microwave oven until the liquid is evaporated and only the butter remains. Add the parsley and cook, covered, for 1 minute.

Add the butter-parsley mixture to the Jerusalem artichokes. Add **177** salt and pepper. Stir to coat evenly and well.

Tip: by adding the liquid to the butter, the water may be evaporated out of the liquid but any nutrients will stay in the butter. This trick may be used with many vegetables.

My Time Is _____ Min.

JERUSALEM ARTICHOKES IN SOUR CREAM

The touch of lemon gives a tang to this dish to offset the slight sweetness of the Jerusalem artichokes. The addition of sour cream and bacon will make this one of your favorites.

Makes 4 servings

1 pound Jerusalem artichokes
1/4 cup water
1/2 cup sour cream
1 tablespoon lemon juice (children may prefer 1/2 tablespoon)

Preparation time 15 Min.

3 slices crisp-cooked bacon
1/2 teaspoon dill weed
Salt and pepper to taste

The bacon may be cooked on several sheets of paper toweling in the microwave oven while the Jerusalem artichokes are being prepared. The bacon will take about 3 minutes cooking time.

178 Peel and dice the Jerusalem artichokes into 1/2-inch cubes. Put it and the water into a covered casserole and cook, stirring several times, in the microwave oven until tender (about 7 minutes).

Mix together the sour cream, lemon juice, bacon, and dill weed. Stir into the casserole. Add salt and pepper to taste.

Tip: stirring is essential to even cooking. This dish may be served hot, as a vegetable, or chilled, as a salad.

My Time Is _____ Min.

LEEKS

The leek, like the onion, is a member of the lily family. It has a very distinctive growth pattern. The leaves come out of either side of a compressed stem. Each leaf is like a wide grass blade and is keeled like the bottom of a ship, so that it looks like it could be folded in two lengthwise.

The bulb, the succulent cylinder of the leaf bases, can be used as green onions are. The green leaves may be used for flavoring. The whole plant may be used as a vegetable or made into soup.

Leeks cannot be stored a long time because they wilt and spoil easily, as do green onions.

Selection

Look for fresh, deep green coloring, young, tender leaves, and a plump, fresh appearance. Select small to medium leeks, if possible, as the larger ones may be old and tough. Avoid limp or raggedy appearing leeks.

Preparation

Leeks are a little difficult to clean—and they really need it as dirt washes down between the leaves. The leaves are balanced, one growing first on one side and then one on the other side. Take a sharp, pointed knife and insert it through the center of the leaves on one side near the base of the leek and out through the center of the leaves on the other side and cut upwards. Pull each leaf downward and, holding the leaf tips down to prevent the washing of more dirt into the base of the leek, wash thoroughly under running water. The leeks can be cooked cut in half or quarters lengthwise, or they can be sliced into pieces crosswise. The roots should be cut off at the base of the bulb. Discard any part of the green leaves that is tough.

Cooking

Fresh

As leeks are sold fresh only, no other cooking instructions are given.

Put the leeks and 2 tablespoons water in a covered casserole. Cook in the microwave oven, stirring twice, until the leeks are tender and done. One-and-one-half pounds (2 bunches) of leeks will cook in about 7 to 8 minutes.

Seasonings:	garlic, lemon, onion, marjoram, parsley, oregano, thyme, butter, salt, pepper
Sauces:	Allemande, Béchamel, Butter and Seed, Cheese, Hollandaise, Hot Poppy Seed, Mornay, Parsley, and Tomato sauces; sour cream
Cheeses:	American, Cheddar, Cottage, Monterey Jack, Mozzarella, Parmesan, Provolone, Ricotta, Romano, Swiss
Wines:	chablis, rhine wine, rosé, sauterne, sherry, vermouth
Nuts:	pine nuts, sunflower seed
Extra serving suggestions:	hot, dressed with lemon, butter, salt, and pepper
	hot, in tomato sauce and covered with mozzarella cheese
	cold, in sour cream mixed with lemon juice, garlic, salt, and pepper

LUSCIOUS LEEKS

Leeks are a good source of calcium and potassium. Leeks are a very mild member of the onion family. Try this tasty version.

Makes 4 servings *(3/4 lb)*
Preparation time 10 Min.

1 bunch leeks
2 tablespoons butter or margarine
2 tablespoons dry onion soup mix

1/2 cup sour cream
Salt and pepper to taste

Cut the leek stalks in half, lengthwise, and wash thoroughly. Drain. Trim. Cut the leeks crosswise in 3/4-inch slices. Put the leeks and the butter in a covered casserole. Cook in the microwave oven, stirring once, until tender (about 5 to 7 minutes). Gently mix the dry onion soup mix and the sour cream. Stir into the leeks. Add the salt and pepper and stir again. Reheat 1 minute, if necessary.

Tip: the combination of dry onion soup mix and sour cream is good, very good, on many vegetables. Use it on any of the "greens" or members of the cabbage family.

181

My Time Is _____ Min.

LEEK SOUP

Serve this soup one of two ways—just as it comes from the microwave oven or put through a blender to make a cream soup. It is good and refreshing, whether served piping hot or chilled.

Makes 6 servings

- 1/4 pound bacon, diced
- 1 cup chopped onion
- 1 cup finely-chopped carrot
- 1 cup finely-chopped celery
- 2 bunches leeks
- 4 medium-sized potatoes, peeled and diced
- 1 tablespoon dried parsley flakes or 1/4 cup fresh parsley
- 1 teaspoon salt

Preparation time 35 Min.

- Pepper to taste
- 1/4 cup dry white wine (optional)
- 1 cup water
- 1 teaspoon chicken bouillon concentrate
- 2 tablespoons flour
- 1 can (13 ounces) evaporated milk
- Water as needed

182 Cook the bacon in a large casserole, uncovered, until it is brown and crisp. (This will take about 4 to 5 minutes.) Discard all but 2 tablespoons of the bacon drippings. Cut the leeks in half lengthwise. Wash them very thoroughly. Cut the leeks in 1/2-inch slices, crosswise, using all the white parts and as much of the green parts as are not too tough and coarse.

Put the bacon, bacon drippings, onion, carrot, celery, leeks, potatoes, parsley, salt, pepper, wine, water, chicken bouillon, and flour in the casserole and cook, covered, in the microwave oven, stirring from time-to-time, until the vegetables are tender. (This should take about 15 to 20 minutes.) Blend in the milk. Add enough water to make 6 cups soup. Heat to a simmer.

Tip: fresh cream may be used, but the evaporated milk actually gives a better flavor, is less expensive, and does not add as many calories.

My Time Is _____ *Min.*

LEEK DISH FROM VAUD

This recipe combines a starch and a succulent vegetable, as well as a protein. Try it for a brunch, a supper, or even with a hearty dinner.

Makes 6 servings   *Preparation time 45 Min.*

4 medium potatoes, peeled and sliced	Dash of pepper
4 large leeks, cut into rings (well cleaned)	1/4 teaspoon dried basil leaves
1 cup beef broth or bouillon	1/4 teaspoon dried thyme leaves
1 tablespoon flour	1/8 teaspoon ground nutmeg
2 tablespoons milk	1/2 pound sliced bacon
1 teaspoon salt	1/2 pound bratwurst sausage

Place the potatoes and leeks in layers in a covered casserole. Add 1/2 cup beef broth. Cook, covered, until almost tender (about 10 to 15 minutes). Stir together the flour, seasonings, and milk. Stir in the remaining beef broth. Pour into the casserole and set aside.

Cook the bacon between paper towels in the microwave oven until browned (about 8 minutes). Place on top of the casserole. Cook the bratwurst sausage in a covered casserole in the microwave oven for 5 minutes. Slice and arrange on top of the bacon. Cook the casserole, covered, 5 minutes more in the microwave oven. Let stand 5 minutes more.

183

Tip: if the leeks are sandy or dirty, it may be necessary to quarter them to clean them thoroughly, in which case it would not be possible to cut them in rings. Use as much of the green tops as possible, but discard any tough or coarse parts.

My Time Is _____ Min.

LENTILS

Lentils take their name from the lens-shaped seeds. They are members of the pea family and are very high in vegetable protein. Lentils were probably one of the first plants cultivated by man. They were known in the Bronze Age, and were even mentioned in the first book, Gen. 25: 30–34, of the Old Testament.

Lentils may be made into a soup, cooked as a bean, used in stews, flavored with bacon or sausage, or cooked (Asian) Indian style with rice.

Cooking of lentils in the microwave oven is a rehydration process and is not done very much faster than it is conventionally; but in the microwave oven there is no chance of burning or scorching, as in conventional cooking. Their growth pattern makes lentils a little hard to clean.

Selection

Lentils come prepackaged so there is no selection.

Preparation

Sort through the lentils to remove any matter that should not be there. It is not too uncommon to find small pieces of rock in dried beans, peas, and lentils. Put the lentils in a colander or sieve and rinse.

Cooking

Put the lentils in a very large, covered casserole. Add enough water to cover the lentils by about 1 inch. Add 1 tablespoon of butter, margarine, or oil. Cook, covered, in the microwave oven. Every 10 minutes, stir. Add more water as is needed. One cup of lentils will absorb 4 cups of water and will take about 35 minutes to cook. If more lentils are added, more cooking time and water will be needed.

Always use a very large casserole and the butter to prevent boiling over. It is wise to set the casserole on a large plate during the cooking period. Any boiled-over liquid will be retained by the plate. This is also why all the water is not added at once. Lentils need 5 minutes standing time.

One cup lentils equals 1/2 pound.

Seasonings:	coriander, cumin (comino), garlic, ginger, mint, mustard, nutmeg, onion, paprika, parsley, poppy seed, scallions, sesame seed, thyme, butter, salt, pepper, sugar, brown sugar, honey, molasses
Sauces:	Cheese, Tomato
Wines:	burgundy, chablis, claret, port, sherry, tokay
Nuts:	pine nuts, sunflower seed

186

BAKED LENTILS

Here is a basic recipe along with a handful of variations. Try them all. They are wonderful ways to help vary your menus.

Makes 6 servings   *Preparation time 40 Min.*
- 1 cup dry lentils
- 4 cups water, to be added as needed
- 3 slices bacon, diced
- 1/4 cup chopped onion
- 1 teaspoon salt

Put all ingredients, except the water, into a covered casserole. Add 2 cups water. Cook 10 minutes in the microwave oven. Stir and add 1 more cup water. Cook 10 minutes more. Stir and add the remaining water. Cook until the lentils are tender. Let stand 5 minutes.

Variations

Use the basic recipe of lentils in place of meat when making vegetarian tacos.

Add 6 tablespoons honey, 1 tablespoon vinegar, and 1 teaspoon dry mustard to the basic recipe.

187

Add 1/2 cup catsup, 1/2 cup brown sugar, and 1 tablespoon vinegar to the basic recipe.

Delete chopped onion and add 2 onions cut into wedges, 2 green peppers cut into strips, 2 tablespoons tomato paste, and 2 teaspoons chili powder for Mexican-style lentils.

Tip: use lentils often in your menus. For a vegetable, they have the most complete source of protein. Vegetarians often use them as a staple in their diet. A little grated cheese stirred into the lentils ensures that the protein will be the same quality as that of steaks or roasts. Lentils can be a big budget helper.

My Time Is _____ *Min.*

LENTILS WITH PINEAPPLE

From Mexico, enjoy a dish that combines lentils and pineapple for a delightfully-different way to serve these nutritious legumes.

Makes 6 servings	*Preparation time 50 Min.*
1 1/2 cups lentils	1/4 cup tomato catsup
3 1/2 cups water	1/2 teaspoon salt
1/2 cup diced bacon	1/8 teaspoon pepper
1/2 cup chopped onion	1 1/2 cups pineapple cubes
1/4 teaspoon powdered thyme	

If possible, soak the lentils overnight in enough water to cover. If not possible, more liquid and more cooking time must be added.

Cook the bacon in a 2-quart casserole in the microwave oven until crisp. Add the onion and thyme. Cook, covered, 4 minutes. Add the catsup, salt, pepper, and lentils. (If using canned pineapple cubes, drain the liquid and use as part of the water which is added to cook the lentils.)

188 Add 2 cups liquid and cook lentils, covered, stirring occasionally, adding more liquid, as needed. Almost all liquid should be absorbed by the time the lentils are tender. (The cooking time should be about 35 minutes.) Add the pineapple cubes. If fresh pineapple is used, cook 10 to 15 minutes or until the pineapple is done.

Tip: set the casserole in a cake or pie dish while cooking the lentils. If there is a boil-over, the liquid is caught in the lower dish and can be poured back into the casserole so that none of the liquid or the flavoring ingredients are lost. While the cooking of lentils is not greatly speeded up in the microwave oven, there is no danger of scorching or burning, as in conventional cooking.

My Time Is _____ Min.

LENTILS AND RICE

From India comes a grain and legume combination that is most tasty. Try it with any meat or curry dish. Lentils are high in vegetable protein.

Makes 8 servings
8 peppercorns
8 cardamom seeds (the black ones inside the white pod)
1 bay leaf
1 piece ginger root

Preparation time 55 Min.
1 cup lentils
3 cups, or more, water
1 large onion, thinly sliced
1 cup raw rice
2 tablespoons oil or butter

Tie the peppercorns, cardamom seeds, bay leaf, and ginger in a piece of clean, washed cheesecloth. Put it into the bottom of a large, covered casserole. Pour in the lentils and 3 cups water. Cook, covered, in the microwave oven for 30 minutes, stirring occasionally. Add the onion, rice, and oil. Cook, covered, 20 minutes more in the microwave oven or until the rice is tender and the water is absorbed, stirring occasionally. If more water is needed before the end of the cooking period, add whatever amount is needed to get the rice tender. Remove and discard the spice bag.

189

Tip: to make the flavor of the seasonings more pronounced, pound with a hammer or a heavy object several times before starting to cook. This will release more of the flavoring oils by bruising the tissues. One white cardamom seed pod usually holds about the right number of seeds for this recipe.

My Time Is _____ *Min.*

LENTILS AND SAUSAGE

Hearty, tasty, nutritious, and economical, this dish is easy to prepare and is certain to become one of your favorites.

Makes 4 servings   *Preparation time 45 Min.*

1/2 pound lentils	2 tomatoes, peeled and chopped
2 tablespoons oil	1 jar (2 ounces) sliced pimientos
3 cups water or more as needed	1 clove garlic, minced
3 chipolata sausages (or chorizo) cut into pieces	1/4 cup minced parsley
1 onion, chopped	Salt and pepper to taste

Put the lentils, oil, and 3 cups water in a large, covered casserole. Set in another dish to catch any boil-over. Cook 20 minutes, stirring several times. If using the chorizo, skin and cut into small pieces. Add sausage and all remaining ingredients to the lentils. If the lentils are getting too dry, add up to 1 more cup water. Cook, covered, in the microwave oven, another 20 minutes, stirring from time-to-time. Let stand 10 to 15 minutes.

190 **Tip:** the lentils should have a small amount of liquid left when the cooking is done, but should not be soupy. The cooking of lentils is not greatly speeded up in the microwave oven, but this is offset by the fact that they do not scorch or burn if they get too dry.

My Time Is _____ Min.

MUSHROOMS

The mushroom is the fruiting body of certain underground fungi. The part that is eaten is called a sporophore, which consists of the cap and the stem. In general, the term mushroom is used to mean the edible, non-poisonous sporophores, while the term toadstool refers to the poisonous forms. Unless you have been very well trained to know and recognize both types of fungi, do not attempt to harvest wild "mushrooms." As expensive as they are in the market, they are cheap when compared to risking your life.

In choosing mushrooms in the market, look for those with closed caps and short stems. Closed caps mean the mushroom is young and succulent and will keep a little longer. Also, the gills are not exposed so dirt has not gotten into them.

Short stems mean you will get more mushroom caps per pound. The stems are dense, and sometimes woody, and weigh heavy.

Selection

First, look for tightly-closed caps, an indication of young mushrooms which will keep longer. Also, dirt hasn't had a chance to work into the gills if the cap hasn't opened. The cap should be plump and without any feeling of sliminess. Look for mushrooms whose stems were cut short. Stems weigh heavier than caps. The caps are the most desirable part for eating.

Preparation

Wash gently and drain. If the mushrooms are to be used whole, they are now ready. If the mushrooms are to be stuffed, gently pull the stem loose and out; then stuff. The mushrooms may also be sliced or chopped, according to the demands of the recipe.

Cooking

Fresh

Put the mushrooms and 1 teaspoon butter, margarine, or oil in a covered casserole. Cook in the microwave oven, stirring twice, until the mushrooms are tender. One-half pound of mushrooms will cook in about 10 to 12 minutes.

Frozen

Put the mushrooms in a covered casserole. If they are frozen in a block, put the icy-side up. Cook in the microwave oven, stirring twice, until the mushrooms are hot and tender (about 7 minutes for a 6-ounce package).

Canned

Canned mushrooms are fully cooked, therefore, they only need heating.

Seasonings:	dill, garlic, lemon, marjoram, onion, oregano, paprika, parsley, rosemary, sesame seed, thyme, butter, salt, pepper
Sauces:	Allemande, Bearnaise, Béchamel, Hot Poppy Seed, Mornay, and Parsley sauces; sour cream
Cheeses:	Blue, Cream, Gruyère, Monterey Jack, Parmesan, Romano, Swiss
Wines:	burgundy, chablis, claret, rhine wine, rosé, sauterne, sherry, vermouth
Nuts:	almonds, pecans, pine nuts, pistachios, pumpkin seed, sunflower seed, walnuts, water chestnuts
Extra serving suggestions:	hot, with butter, salt, pepper, and Parmesan cheese
	hot, in an omelet
	hot, with wine, Parmesan cheese, marjoram, thyme, butter, salt, and pepper
	cooked in butter, chilled, and stirred into sour cream with lemon juice and dill weed added

MUSHROOM AND ASPARAGUS SALAD

Here is a tossed salad utilizing some cooked and some raw produce. Use your microwave oven to cook the asparagus so as to retain its lovely color, nutrients, and flavor.

Makes 6 servings

4 tablespoons butter or oil
1/2 pound mushrooms, thickly sliced
1/2 pound asparagus spears, cut into 1-inch pieces
4 medium tomatoes, peeled and cut into wedges
1 green pepper, seeded and cut into strips

Preparation time 20 Min.

4 tiny sweet pickles, sliced
1 head Boston lettuce, torn into pieces
2 tablespoons wine vinegar
1 teaspoon salt
Pepper to taste

Put the butter, mushrooms, and all but the tender tip pieces of the asparagus in a covered casserole and cook, covered, 5 minutes, stirring occasionally. Add the tips and cook, covered, 3 minutes more. Chill. Add all the other ingredients and toss well. Serve immediately.

193

Tip: if the tender asparagus tips were cooked as long as the rest of the spears, they would be mushy. Note the beautiful color contrast of the asparagus and the tomatoes.

My Time Is _____ Min.

CHINESE STUFFED MUSHROOMS

These can be a rich, filling hors d'oeuvre or a side dish to a meal. Either way they are marvelous and they have that distinctive Oriental flavor.

Makes 4 servings   *Preparation time 25 Min.*

1 pound mushroom caps, 1 1/2 to 2 inches across	1/2 teaspoon salt
	1/2 teaspoon sugar
1 pound ground pork	2 teaspoons cornstarch
1/2 cup finely-chopped water chestnuts	1/2 teaspoon chicken bouillon concentrate
1 tablespoon soy sauce	1/2 cup water
1 tablespoon sherry wine	1/4 cup bottled oyster sauce

Wash the mushrooms and drain them thoroughly. Remove the stems carefully so as to not break the caps. Reserve stems for use elsewhere. Put the ground pork in a covered casserole and cook in the microwave oven for 3 minutes. Break up the pork as finely as possible and continue cooking until all traces of pinkness are gone, stirring from time-to-time. Drain off the excess fat. Mix in the water chestnuts, soy sauce, wine, salt, sugar, and cornstarch.

194

Divide the filling among the mushrooms, filling each cap. Place, cup-side up, in a large rectangular (12″ × 9″) baking dish. Mix the chicken bouillon concentrate, water, and oyster sauce. Pour into the bottom of the baking dish around the caps. Cover with wax paper and cook in the microwave oven until the caps are tender (about 15 minutes).

Tip: cooking the pork first ensures that it is well done without risking overcooking the mushrooms. The mushrooms should still hold their shape and have some texture left after cooking. The sauce can be thickened by mixing in 2 teaspoons of cornstarch before adding it to the dish, in which case the sauce should be stirred twice during the cooking period.

My Time Is _____ Min.

CHICKEN STUFFED MUSHROOMS

From France, here is one of the most delicious hors d'oeuvres you can envision. For a party, you will want to make up several trays ahead of time, to be reheated for the occasion. This tasty morsel can make your reputation as a hostess.

Makes about 24 pieces   *Preparation time 20 Min.*

1 pound mushrooms (about 24 1 1/2- to 2-inch buttons)	1/3 cup chopped pecans
	1 can (5 ounces) chicken spread
1/2 cup salad oil (optional)	2 tablespoons sherry wine
1/2 cup chopped mushroom stems (from above caps)	1 tablespoon salad oil
	1 egg
1/4 cup chopped chives or scallions	1/2 teaspoon salt
	Dash pepper

Wash and drain the mushrooms. Remove the stems from the caps and chop stems. Reserve 1/2 cup for this recipe (remainder may be used elsewhere). This next step is optional. Put oil in a custard cup or other small container. Dip each cap in the oil to coat well. With, or without, the oil bath, put the caps in a 12″ × 9″ rectangular baking dish, cup-side up. For even cooking, put the larger caps in the corners and along the outer edges and the smaller caps in the center of the dish.

195

Mix the remaining ingredients well and fill the mushroom caps, mounding the mixture up until all of it is distributed. Cover with wax paper or plastic wrap and cook 15 minutes. Let stand 5 minutes before serving.

Tip: when cooking irregularly-shaped pieces of food or pieces of food of varying sizes, put the heavier part of each piece, or the larger pieces, around the outer perimeter, and put the largest pieces of all in the corners. In microwave cooking this is where the fastest cooking takes place. Put the thinner parts and smaller pieces on the inside, where the slower cooking takes place. In this manner, you will equalize the cooking time.

My Time Is _____ Min.

FINNISH BAKED MUSHROOMS

These mushrooms in an unsweetened custard-like sauce can be used as a vegetable or as an accompaniment to meat or fish.

Makes 6 servings

- 1/4 cup fine, dry bread crumbs
- 1 tablespoon butter or margarine
- 1 pound mushrooms
- 1 tablespoon lemon juice
- 2 tablespoons finely-minced onion

Preparation time 20 Min.

- 1/4 cup butter or margarine
- Salt and pepper to taste
- 2 cups heavy cream
- 3 tablespoons flour
- 4 egg yolks, lightly beaten

Mix the bread crumbs and 1 tablespoon butter, and toast the bread crumbs in the microwave oven until golden brown, stirring often to prevent burning. Wash and trim the mushrooms and slice thinly. Add the lemon juice, onion, butter, salt, and pepper. Cook, covered, 5 minutes in the microwave oven.

196 Heat the cream in the microwave oven, in a separate covered dish, to just short of the boiling point. Stir the flour into the mushrooms, stirring rapidly to prevent lumping. Stir in a bit of the cream. Stir in each egg yolk separately. Stir in the remaining cream. Cook, covered, in the microwave oven until the sauce is just short of boiling. Sprinkle with the toasted bread crumbs and let stand 5 minutes before serving.

Tip: the thicker the cream, the better this dish tastes. Half and half is better than milk, and whipping cream is best of all; but let your purse and your waistline be your guide.

My Time Is _____ Min.

MUSHROOMS STUFFED WITH GUACAMOLE

Whether an hors d'oeuvre or a vegetable, this is "out of this world" for flavor. A bit on the expensive side but worth every penny!

Makes about 24 pieces   *Preparation time 20 Min.*

- 1 pound fresh, whole mushroom caps
- 1 large or 2 small ripe avocados
- 2 tablespoons very finely-minced onion
- 2 cloves garlic, very finely minced
- 1/3 cup finely-chopped fresh tomato
- 2 teaspoons lemon juice
- 2 dashes of liquid hot pepper sauce (or to taste)
- Salt to taste
- 6 slices cooked, crumbled bacon or 1/2 cup toasted sunflower seed

Wash, dry, and stem the mushrooms. Place them, cup-side up, in a 2-quart (12" × 9") casserole or baking dish. Put the biggest mushrooms in the corners of the dish and the smallest ones along the center of the dish. Cover and cook in the microwave oven for 15 minutes or until tender. Meanwhile, peel, seed, and thoroughly mash the avocado. Blend in the onion, garlic, tomato, lemon juice, hot pepper sauce, and salt. When the mushrooms are cooked, divide the guacamole filling among them according to size. Top with either the crumbled bacon or the sunflower seed. Serve.

197

Tip: putting the bigger mushrooms in the corners allows them to cook faster. Putting the smaller mushrooms in the center allows them to cook more slowly. This way all the mushrooms cook in the same amount of time.

My Time Is _____ *Min.*

MUSHROOMS IN MADEIRA SAUCE

These mushrooms are the perfect accompaniment to a steak or a thick slice of roast. Wow! This is no ordinary-tasting sauce.

Makes 3 cups *Preparation time 23 Min.*

1/2 pound mushrooms, washed and sliced	1 teaspoon Kitchen Bouquet
2 tablespoons butter	1/2 teaspoon salt
1/2 cup chopped green onion	1/8 teaspoon thyme
3 tablespoons butter	1 tablespoon tomato paste (or 1/4 cup tomato sauce)
3 tablespoons flour	
2 teaspoons (or 2 cubes) beef bouillon concentrate	2 cups water
	1/4 cup Madeira wine

Put the mushrooms and 2 tablespoons butter in a covered casserole and cook in the microwave oven for 5 minutes. Stir in the green onion. Cook, covered, 1 minute more in the microwave oven. Set aside.

198 Melt the butter in a 1-quart casserole. Stir in the flour, bouillon concentrate, Kitchen Bouquet, salt, thyme, and tomato paste. Gradually blend in the water. Stir in the wine. Cook, covered, in the microwave oven until the mixture comes to a boil (about 6 minutes), stirring from time-to-time during the last 4 minutes. When the sauce has thickened and come to a boil, continue cooking for 3 minutes more on defrost or low power. If these powers are not available, let the sauce sit for 2 minutes and then cook 1 minute more on high. Stir in the mushrooms and onions and cook, covered, 1 minute to reheat.

Tip: adding the onions so late in the cooking time allows them to retain more of their bright green color accent. It also allows them to retain more of their fresh taste. If more of a cooked taste is desired, they can be added earlier in the cooking process.

My Time Is _____ *Min.*

MUSHROOM PARMESAN

Serve these at a party or with a festive dinner. You may want to prepare several batches ahead of time, as they freeze well. Just a few minutes of reheating and they are piping hot for the times you have impromptu guests.

Makes about 24 pieces

1 pound fresh mushroom caps
1/3 cup butter, melted
1/8 teaspoon garlic powder
1/4 teaspoon powdered oregano

Preparation time 20 Min.

Salt and pepper to taste
1/2 cup grated Parmesan cheese

Wash the mushrooms, remove the stems, and drain well. Melt the butter in a custard cup. Stir in the garlic powder, oregano, salt, and pepper. Dip each mushroom in the butter to coat well. Place in a single layer in a 2-quart rectangular (12″ × 9″) baking dish. Cook, uncovered, 15 minutes, or until tender, stirring several times. Sprinkle on Parmesan cheese and stir to coat well. Let stand 5 minutes.

199

Tip: choose all "caps" that either have not opened or are barely beginning to open, as they break apart less easily. Also, for uniform cooking, choose all caps as near the same size as possible. Save the stems to be used in a dish that requires chopped mushrooms.

My Time Is _____ Min.

MUSHROOMS IN SOUR CREAM

Whether you need an hors d'oeuvre or an accompaniment for meat, this is a good choice. It is elegant, yet very easy to prepare. Good, good, good.

Makes about 24 pieces

Preparation time 25 Min.

- 1 pound mushrooms (about 24 1 1/2- to 2-inch buttons)
- 1/4 cup chopped onion
- 1/2 teaspoon dill weed
- 1/4 cup chopped parsley
- 1/4 cup butter or margarine
- 1 cup sour cream
- 2 tablespoons sherry wine
- Salt and pepper to taste

Wash, stem, and drain the mushroom caps. Put the mushrooms, onion, dill weed, parsley and butter in a 2-quart covered casserole. Cook, covered, 15 minutes, stirring several times. Let stand 5 minutes. Add the sour cream, wine, salt, and pepper. Reheat, but *do not* let boil.

Tip: prepare several batches and freeze for unexpected guests. These freeze well. They also make a nice topping to put over sliced roast beef and other dishes. For a slightly different taste, substitute sage for the dill weed.

200

My Time Is _____ Min.

OKRA

Okra is an herbaceous plant of the mallow family and grows only in tropical and sub-tropical areas. The tender, unripe, fruit is eaten and prepared much as asparagus is. This fruit is called gumbo, hence the name gumbo is also given to those same dishes which are popular in the deep South.

Due to its high content of mucilage, okra is used for the thickening of broths and soups.

The seeds are used as a "coffee" in some countries and made into necklaces in others.

Selection

Fresh okra is not commonly found in most markets outside of the South and Texas, except for areas where there are large pockets of Southern emigrants.

Look for pods that are 2 to 4 inches long. Larger pods will be tough and woody. Avoid any vegetable that has shriveled or yellowed.

Preparation

Wash and drain the okra. Cut off the stems. The fruit may be used whole, sliced, or diced.

Cooking

Fresh

Put the okra and 1/4 cup water in a covered casserole. Cook in the microwave oven until tender, stirring once. One-half pound of okra should cook in about 5 to 6 minutes.

One of the common ways of preparing okra, frying it, cannot be done in the microwave oven.

Frozen

Put the okra and 2 tablespoons water in a covered casserole. Cook in the microwave oven, stirring once, until tender. A 10-ounce package should take 6 to 7 minutes to cook.

Canned

Canned okra is fully cooked and only needs heating before using.

Seasonings:	lemon, onion, salt, pepper
Sauce:	Tomato
Wines:	chablis, sauterne, dry vermouth

202

OKRA AND TOMATOES

If you are a lover of okra, try this combination. If you have any leftover cooked ham, add 1/2 cup of it, chopped into tiny pieces, right in with the onions. If you have some shrimp on hand, add it with the tomatoes.

Makes 6 servings	*Preparation time 10 Min.*
1/4 cup chopped onion	2 tablespoons water
2 tablespoons butter	2 medium tomatoes,
Dash or two of cayenne	chopped (about 1 1/2
1 package (10 ounces)	cups)
frozen whole okra	Salt to taste

Put the onion, butter, and cayenne in a covered casserole. Cook in the microwave oven for 3 minutes. Add the okra and water. Cook, covered, stirring twice, until the okra is tender (about 6 to 7 minutes). Add the tomatoes and salt. Stir. Cook, covered, about 1 1/2 minutes or until the tomatoes are heated through. Let stand 3 minutes. Serve.

Tip: the okra may be sliced after 3 minutes of cooking. That is just long enough to allow you to separate the okra pods. If you are **203** a first time okra eater, try them whole.

My Time Is _____ Min.

OKRA CUSTARD PARMESAN

People usually either love or hate okra. If you love okra, or if this is your first time to try it, this is a good recipe. Actually, people like the flavor of okra, it tastes a lot like green beans; it is the texture that is objected to and the custard helps disguise it.

Makes 4 servings

- 1 package (10 ounces) frozen whole okra
- 2 tablespoons water
- 1 cup milk
- 1 egg, beaten
- 1 teaspoon basil leaves, crushed

Preparation time 12 Min.

- 1/4 cup cracker crumbs
- 1/4 cup grated Parmesan cheese

Salt and pepper to taste

Put the okra and water into a covered casserole. Cook in the microwave oven 3 minutes. Rearrange the okra pods, putting any that feel cool to the outer edge. Cook 3 minutes longer.

204 Meanwhile, beat the milk into the eggs. Stir in the basil, cracker crumbs, Parmesan cheese, salt, and pepper. Pour over the okra. Cook 3 minutes, covered. Stir gently to mix the more cooked parts of the custard with those that are less cooked. Smooth over the top so that the okra is covered with the sauce. Cook, covered, 3 minutes more.

Tip: for a change of flavor, add 1/4 cup chopped onion in with the frozen okra. Take care to not overcook the okra. It needs a bit of crispness left to improve the texture.

My Time Is _____ Min.

ONIONS

The onion is a hardy, biennial plant of the lily family. There are two types of onions, those that form seeds and those that are propagated by bulblet divisions or by division of the plant cluster. Onions are grown the world over and are used in all types of cuisines.

Some onions are started from seed and some from "sets," the tiny little onions started the previous year from seed. Many kinds of onions need special growing requirements and so only grow in specific parts of the world.

Choose the type of onion that you like. Some kinds are very *hot* and pungent. The Bermuda onion is a *very mild* onion but does not keep very long. The Maui onion is probably the sweetest onion of all. It is hard to imagine cooking without this lowly bulb.

Selection

Look for firm, well-shaped onions. Onions that are soft are on their way to spoiling. Onions that have spoiled areas will have a great deal of waste and the flavor of the remaining onion may be affected. Choose boiling onions of a uniform size.

Preparation

Cut off the end of the neck of the onion. Remove the skin by slitting it from top to bottom and then pulling it off. Whether to remove the tiny core at the root end depends on how the onion is to be used. If the onion is to be cut into wedges and should remain intact, leave it. If you want the onion to separate into segments, remove it.

Rinse and drain the onions. If the onion is to be cooked whole, it is ready. The onion may be cut into wedges, sliced, or chopped.

Cooking

Fresh

If onions are to be cooked whole, put them in a covered casserole. Cook until tender in the microwave oven. Halfway through the cooking period, give each onion a half turn. Two onions take about 5 to 7 minutes to cook, 4 onions take about 7 to 9 minutes, and 6 onions take 10 to 12 minutes.

Sliced or chopped onions cook in about the same time span. The only difference is that they should be stirred twice during the cooking period.

Whole boiling onions also need stirring twice during the cooking period. One pound of boiling onions will cook in about 7 to 8 minutes.

Frozen

Whole boiling onions are the ones commonly frozen. Put them in a covered casserole and cook in the microwave oven until they are tender. If some of the onions are a bit larger than the others, it is best to put them in the casserole alone and cook them about 2 minutes before adding the smaller onions. Stir twice during the cooking period. A 10-ounce package of boiling onions will cook in 8 to 10 minutes.

Canned

Canned onions are fully cooked and therefore only need heating before using.

Seasonings:	chervil, clove, dill, fennel, garlic, ginger, lemon, mint, nutmeg, oregano, paprika, parsley, poppy seed, sage, savory, sesame seed, thyme, butter, salt, pepper
Sauces:	Allemande, Bearnaise, Béchamel, Butter and Seed, Cheese, Hollandaise, Hot Poppy Seed, Mornay, Parsley, Tomato, Velouté, and White sauces; sour cream
Cheeses:	American, Cheddar, Gruyère, Monterey Jack, Mozzarella, Parmesan, Provolone, Ricotta, Romano, Swiss
Wines:	chablis, rhine wine, rosé, sauterne, sherry, vermouth

Nuts:	almonds, filberts, pine nuts, pistachios, pumpkin seed, sunflower seed, water chestnuts
Extra serving suggestions:	hot, with a White sauce with mint and parsley, and sprinkled with pine nuts
	sliced and cooked with butter, salt, pepper, and sunflower seed
	hot, with Mornay sauce and crumbled bacon on top
	hot, in a Velouté sauce with rosé wine and nutmeg
	hot, in a Mornay sauce and sprinkled with poppy seed

Onions cooked in the microwave oven are so sweet and flavorful, it is difficult to equate them with the onions that come from conventional cooking. Here is a recipe that brings you two vegetables in one colorful, appealing dish—to be made ahead of time and chilled. Plan this for the day when you will come home late and have to rush dinner to the table.

Makes 6 servings   *Preparation time 25 Min.*

6 medium-sized onions	1/4 teaspoon salt
3/4 cup olive oil	1/8 teaspoon pepper
1/4 cup lemon juice	1 green pepper
1/2 teaspoon powdered dry mustard	1 cup water
	Paprika as needed

208

Cut off and discard the top and bottom slices from the onions. Peel the onions and score them, cutting 1/3 of the way from the top in two cuts made at right angles to each other. Place in a covered casserole and cook in the microwave oven until tender (about 8 to 10 minutes). Blend the oil, lemon juice, and seasonings. Pour over the onions and chill well. Occasionally, baste the onions with the lemon juice-oil mixture, for a better blending of flavors.

Bring 1 cup water to a boil in a 2-cup measure in the microwave oven. Cut and seed the green pepper and cut into long strips. Drop into the water and cook for 1 minute. Use as garnish with the onions. Top with paprika.

Tip: the green pepper can be cut into quarters and seeded before dropping into the water and cooking for 1 minute. Then peel before cutting into strips. It is a nice, but not essential, touch. Some people will like the pepper cooked a little longer, but it should still have a crisp texture to contrast with the onion.

My Time Is _____ Min.

BAKED STUFFED ONIONS

Onions cooked in the microwave oven are so sweet and mild it is hard to think of them as onions. Here the filling and the onion are perfect flavor blends for each other.

Makes 6 servings

Preparation time 20 Min.

- 6 medium-large onions
- 1 1/2 cups Ricotta or small curd Cottage cheese
- 2 eggs, beaten
- 1 teaspoon salt
  Pepper to taste
- 2 teaspoons dried parsley flakes
- 1/2 teaspoon basil leaves, crushed
- 1/4 teaspoon nutmeg

Slice off tops and bottoms of onions. Peel them. Cook in a circle in a covered casserole in the microwave oven for 5 minutes. Turn each onion a half turn. Cook, covered, 5 minutes more. Hold in a hot pad or towel and gently remove the center of each onion, leaving a fairly thick outer wall of onion. Cut a piece of the onion that has been removed and put it in the bottom of each opening so the filling will not run through. Beat the remaining ingredients until smooth and well mixed. Divide between the onions, filling to the top. Cook, covered, in the microwave oven about 3 minutes more, or until the filling is heated through, but not long enough to cause it to "boil over." May be garnished with a sprig of parsley.

209

Tip: the onion that has been removed from the center may be used any way you please. It may be chopped and added to dishes needing chopped onion, or it may be added, as is, to stews. Cooked onion may be safely frozen until needed.

My Time Is _____ Min.

PARSNIPS

The parsnip is a member of the carrot family. It is native to Europe and has been cultivated since the time of the Romans. It looks like a large white carrot but is a little broader at the top of the root and then narrows quickly. Colonists brought it to the New World over 300 years ago.

At the end of the growing season the root is high in starch and not yet well flavored. After the first frosts, enzymes in the root change the starch to sugar and make it sweet and flavorful. The parsnip can be left in the soil during the winter and dug up in small batches whenever the soil thaws.

The parsnip has a very pervasive flavor. If it is to be used in stews, it is advisable to cook it separately and combine it with the rest of the food just before serving. Otherwise, everything tastes of parsnip.

Selection

Select parsnips that are firm and without blemishes. Also try to select those that are smooth, as they are easier to peel. Those that are very large at the top are apt to be easier to cook, as nice large slices are available. When possible, avoid those with brown or soft spots. Parsnips harvested after the first heavy frost or freeze will be much sweeter than those harvested earlier. If you raise your own, leave most of them in the ground during the winter and harvest them when they are needed or when the ground thaws from time-to-time.

Preparation

Pare the parsnips. Remove the center of the top until only creamy, white flesh remains. If the tip of the root is blemished, cut it off. The root may be cooked whole, halved, or quartered, or it may be cut into slices or diced. When slicing, try to have the same amount of vegetable in each piece. Start at the top and slice thinly. As the root gets smaller and smaller, cut the slices thicker and thicker.

Cooking

Fresh

As parsnips are usually available fresh only, no other cooking suggestions are given.

If the parsnips are to be cooked whole, halved, or quartered, use a loaf pan and put half of the large ends of the pieces to one end of the dish and the other half with the large ends to the other end of the dish. Overlap the thin ends as much as possible. Add 1/4 cup water. Cover with plastic wrap or wax paper. Cook, re-arranging the pieces once, covered in the microwave oven until tender. It takes about 8 to 10 minutes for 1 pound. When re-arranging the pieces put those in the middle of the dish to the out-side and those on the outside to the middle to allow even cooking.

If the parsnips are to be cooked sliced, put them and 1/4 cup water in a covered casserole. Cook, covered, in the microwave oven until they are tender, about 8 to 10 minutes for 1 pound. Stir after 4 and 6 minutes cooking respectively. If, at the end of 6 minutes, some of the bigger pieces are definitely less tender than others, place them around the outer edge of the dish and pile the more tender pieces in the center.

212

If the parsnips are to be cooked diced, put them and 1/4 cup water in a covered casserole and cook in the microwave oven, stirring several times, until tender. This should take about 7 to 9 minutes for 1 pound.

Seasonings:	nutmeg, butter, salt, pepper, sugar
Sauces:	Butter and Seed, Hot Poppy Seed, Tomato

FRIED PARSNIPS

Here is an easy way to fix parsnips that is as old as the hills but converted to your microwave—which is not as old as the hills. Use a browning tray, browning unit, or finish on top of your range.

Makes 4 servings   Preparation time 15 Min.
1 pound parsnips   2 tablespoons butter or
1/4 cup water   more as needed

Peel the parsnips. Then cut them into slices. Start at the largest end of the root. Make the first slices about 3/8-inch thick. As the root gets smaller and smaller, make the slices thicker and thicker so that about the same amount of vegetable is in each piece. Put the parsnips and water in a covered casserole. Cook in the microwave oven, stirring after 4 and 6 minutes respectively, until the parsnips are tender. (This takes about 8 minutes.) Drain the parsnips well and set aside.

Heat your browning tray in the microwave oven until it is as hot as possible. Add the butter and melt. Lay the parsnips in a single layer on the tray. Cook 1 minute (or until lightly browned) on one side. Cook 1 1/2 minutes (or until lightly browned) on the other side. Serve.

213

If your oven has a browning element, stir the butter into the drained parsnips to coat them. Lay in a single layer and brown lightly on one side under the browning element. Turn and lightly brown the other side. Serve.

If your oven does not have a browning tray or cannot take one, melt the butter in a skillet or frying pan on your range top. Brown both sides of the parsnips in the pan. Serve.

Tip: when using a browning tray, use the shorter cooking time on the first side and the longer cooking time on the second side as the tray is cooler then and takes longer to brown. If your family has never eaten parsnips before, this is a good recipe to use for a starter. Parsnips have a rich, slightly sweet flavor that is most enjoyable.

My Time Is _____ Min.

GLAZED PARSNIPS

Parsnips have a sweet, hearty flavor that is most pleasant. You may serve them in place of sweet potatoes, carrots, or winter squash.

Makes 4 servings	*Preparation time 15 Min.*
1 pound parsnips	2 tablespoons butter
1/4 cup water	Dash or two of cinnamon
1/4 cup brown sugar, packed (or 1/4 cup honey)	

Peel the parsnips, then cut them into slices. Start at the largest end of the root. Make the first slices about 3/8-inch thick. As the root gets smaller and smaller, make the slices thicker and thicker so that about the same amount of vegetable is in each piece. Put the parsnips and water in a covered casserole. Cook in the microwave oven, stirring after 4 and 6 minutes respectively, until the parsnips are tender. (This takes about 8 minutes.) Drain the water from the parsnips into a small dish or casserole. Set the parsnips aside.

214 Add the brown sugar (or honey), butter, and cinnamon to the water that has been drained from the parsnips. Cook, uncovered, in the microwave oven, about 3 minutes, until the mixture is about as thick as a medium syrup.

Add the brown sugar mixture to the parsnips and stir very gently to coat each piece. Return to the microwave oven. Cook, uncovered, 1 minute more.

Tip: use the honey in place of the brown sugar as a change of flavor or if your diet does not include refined sugars. Honey is slightly sweeter than brown sugar so a little less may be used, if you desire.

My Time Is _____ Min.

PARSNIPS À LA GREQUE

The sauce gives a tang to contrast delightfully with the sweetness of the parsnips. When possible, make this ahead of time and then either reheat or serve chilled. Standing allows the flavors to blend.

Makes 4 servings

Preparation time 15 Min.

- 1 pound parsnips
- 3/4 cup water
- 3/4 teaspoon chicken bouillon concentrate
- 1 tablespoon lemon juice
- 2 teaspoons wine vinegar
- 1 teaspoon minced parsley
- 1 clove garlic
- 2 tablespoons olive oil
- Pinch dried tarragon leaves, crumbled
- 20 fennel seeds (approximately), crushed
- Salt and pepper to taste

Pare, wash, and slice the parsnips. Put all the ingredients in a covered casserole, except the salt and pepper, and cook in the microwave oven, stirring several times, until the parsnips are tender (about 8 to 12 minutes). Remove the clove of garlic. Add the salt and pepper. Let stand as long as possible before serving. If needed, reheat. May also be served chilled.

215

Tip: when stirring vegetables, stir so as to move the cooler food at the center of the dish to the outside and the outer, hotter food to the inside. This allows the food to cook more evenly.

My Time Is _____ Min.

PARSNIP PATTIES

Try parsnip patties in three different flavors; plain, nutmeg, or onion. You will be tempted to eat them all yourself, but use control. Share them with your family.

Makes 6 patties

Preparation time 20 Min.

1 pound parsnips	1 egg, beaten lightly
2 teaspoons finely-minced onion (use only for onion-flavored patties)	1/8 teaspoon nutmeg (use only for nutmeg-flavored patties)
1/4 cup water	Salt and pepper to taste
1/4 cup liquid (mostly milk)	Butter or margarine
3 tablespoons flour	

Pare, wash, and slice the parsnips. Put them and the onion (if used) and water in a covered casserole. Cook the parsnips in the microwave oven, stirring twice, until the parsnips will mash easily (about 8 minutes). Drain the water from the parsnips into a small microwave-proof bowl. Return to the oven and reduce the liquid to about 1 tablespoon.

216 Use the reduced water as part of the liquid and add enough milk to make 1/4 cup. Mix the milk and the remaining ingredients, except the butter, into the parsnips and beat smooth. Heat the butter until it bubbles in a large, flat dish. Divide the parsnip mixture into six parts. Drop by spoonfuls into the hot butter and with the back of the spoon, mash into a patty form. Cook 1 1/2 minutes on one side. Turn over and cook 45 seconds on the other side. Usually three patties are cooked at one time. Drain on paper toweling.

Tip: if you have a browning tray for your oven, these patties can be cooked on it. Use enough butter to prevent sticking.

My Time Is _____ *Min.*

PEAS

There are many plants in the pea family but only a few are used for food. The pea is a legume which is grown for its edible seed. Peas have been grown for food by man since the Bronze Age. They probably originated as a food in Asia.

Today the picking of peas is a machine job. Most canned or frozen peas are processed within a few hours of picking. Still, there is something nostalgic about sitting and shelling peas. It can be a soothing, relaxing chore in today's hectic life. It is well worth the while to occasionally buy fresh peas in the shell and prepare them yourself. It is better yet when there is someone to share the job with.

In addition to the garden pea common in many cuisines, there is also the edible pod pea variety from the Orient, sometimes called the sugar pea or the snow pea. These pods are picked very young, before the peas get a chance to grow large.

Another type of pea is the chick pea, also known as the garbonzo bean. It is a dry pea.

A smooth pea variety is grown especially to make dried peas used for split pea soup.

Selection

One pound of commercially raised peas-in-the-pod will yield approximately 1 cup shelled peas, maybe a little more. Home-grown peas, which will usually be picked a bit sooner, will probably yield no more than 1 cup of peas. Allow 1/2 pound peas-in-the-pod per serving.

Select fresh green looking pods. If the pods are too light in color and too plump, the peas will be very mature. The younger the peas, the better the flavor and the more tender they are. The French use very tiny immature peas called *Petite Pois,* the ultimate in peas.

Preparation

Open the pods along their curved side and with a finger tip remove the peas. The pods, of course, are discarded. Rinse and drain the peas.

Cooking

Fresh

Put 2 cups peas and 1/4 cup water in a covered casserole. Cook in the microwave oven until tender, stirring twice. The peas will cook in 7 to 8 minutes.

Frozen

Put a 10-ounce package of peas and 2 tablespoons water in a covered casserole. If the peas are frozen into a block, put them icy-side up. Cook in the microwave oven, stirring twice, until tender (about 4 to 6 minutes).

Canned

Canned peas are fully cooked, therefore they only need heating.

Seasonings:	basil, marjoram, nutmeg, onion, savory, butter, salt, pepper, sugar, honey
Sauces:	Allemande, Béchamel, Butter and Seed, Hollandaise, Hot Poppy Seed, Parsley, Velouté, White
Cheeses:	Bel Paise, Cream
Wines:	chablis, rhine wine, sauterne
Extra serving suggestions:	hot, with butter, onion, salt, pepper, and a touch of sugar
	hot, in Parsley sauce with potatoes
	hot, with Butter and Seed sauce using toasted sesame seed
	hot, with bits of onion, mushroom, and celery in Parsley sauce

218

SNOW PEAS (EDIBLE POD PEAS)

Selection

Try to find peas that are slim and flat and that are a good clear green. Avoid those that have yellowed, shriveled, and gone limp.

Preparation

Wash and drain the snow peas. Put your left thumb nail (if you are right handed) against the pea, about 1/8 inch in from the stem end. Grasp the stem end and pull it back against your thumb nail to remove the stem end and any strings that there may be. Strings can form along both sides of snow peas. The peas may be cooked whole or cut.

Cooking

Fresh

Put the peas and 1 tablespoon of butter or margarine into a covered casserole. Cook in the microwave oven, stirring once or twice, depending on the amount being cooked, until tender. One-half pound peas cooks in about 5 minutes. One pound peas takes about 6 to 8 minutes cooking time.

Frozen

Put the frozen peas, icy-side up, in a covered casserole with 1 tablespoon butter or margarine. Cook in the microwave oven until tender, stirring twice. A 6-ounce package will cook in about 5 minutes.

Canned

Snow peas are not usually available canned. If they were, they would be fully cooked and only need heating.

BLACK EYE PEAS

Preparation

Open the outer pod and remove the seeds. The pods are not edible and should be discarded. The beans may be rinsed and then are ready for use. Allow about 3 ounces per serving.

Cooking

Fresh

The maturity, the water content, and the amount of starch in the peas will greatly affect the cooking time and the amount of water needed in the cooking. If the peas are produced commercially, the chances are high that they will be quite mature. In such cases these peas must be treated almost like a dry pea in that they must be covered with water and a relatively long cooking time is needed. A pound of shelled peas will take up to 3 cups water and will cook about 30 to 45 minutes.

If you grow your own peas, you may pick them when they are younger and more tender. If so, less water and a shorter cooking time will be used.

Frozen

Because of the high starch and low water content of frozen black eye peas, there is no appreciable difference in the cooking times and techniques from the fresh beans. A 10-ounce package of commercially-frozen peas will take about 2 cups water and will take from 20 to 25 minutes to cook.

Again, if home-grown, home-frozen peas are used, and if they were picked when less mature, the cooking times will be shortened.

Canned

220 Canned beans are precooked and need only be reheated.

PEAS AND ONIONS

Here is a combination that is satisfying to both the eyes and the taste buds. By cooking the vegetables separately, the perfect degree of doneness can be reached.

Makes 4 servings	Preparation time 20 Min.
1/2 cup tiny boiling onions or pickling onions	1 teaspoon butter or margarine
1 teaspoon butter or margarine	Salt and pepper to taste
1 cup fresh peas or 1 10-ounce package frozen peas	

Peel the onions, then rinse and drain them. Put the onions and 1 teaspoon butter in a covered casserole and cook them in the microwave oven until tender (about 5 to 6 minutes). Be certain to stir them once during the cooking period. When done, set aside.

While the onions are cooking, prepare the peas. Put the peas and 1 teaspoon butter in a covered casserole and cook them in the microwave oven until tender, stirring twice during the cooking period. Fresh peas will take about 6 to 7 minutes cooking time while frozen peas take about 4 to 6 minutes.

221

Add the peas to the onions. Add the salt and pepper. Stir gently to mix. If needed, reheat for 1 minute.

Tip: always cook the onions first. They benefit from the standing time that is available while the peas cook. The peas need little, if any, standing time.

My Time Is _____ Min.

SUGARED PEAS

An old-time favorite. The Mason family has been preparing peas this way for generations. Simple and tasty, the children will love them.

Makes 4 servings	Preparation time 15 Min.
1/4 cup chopped onion	1/4 cup water
2 tablespoons butter	1 teaspoon sugar
2 cups peas	Salt and pepper to taste

Put the onion and butter in a covered casserole. Cook in the microwave oven for 4 minutes. Add the peas, water, and sugar. Cook, covered, in the microwave oven, stirring twice, until the peas are tender. Fresh peas will take 7 to 8 minutes. Frozen peas may take a little less time. Canned peas only need heating. Drain the liquid from the peas into a small dish or casserole. Reduce by boiling until only the butter and sugar mixture remains. Pour it over the peas. Add the salt and pepper. Stir gently to mix. Serve.

Tip: if using canned peas, drain most of the liquid from them before using. The liquid may be boiled down and used with the peas as suggested above or may be reserved to use in soups.

My Time Is _____ *Min.*

SNOW PEAS AND TINY ONIONS

The tiny onions take a little time to peel, but the flavor of the combination is more than worth the time spent. The color contrast makes the dish a very pretty sight.

Makes 4 servings

Preparation time 15 Min.

1/2 pound tiny boiling onions
  or pickling onions

1 teaspoon butter or
  margarine

1/2 pound edible pod peas
  (snow peas)

1 teaspoon butter or
  margarine

Salt and pepper to taste

Peel the onions. Put the peeled onions and 1 teaspoon butter in a covered casserole and cook in the microwave oven, stirring once, until the onions are tender (about 5 to 6 minutes). Set aside.

While the onions are cooking, prepare the peas by snapping off the stem and pulling off the strings. Rinse and drain. Put the edible pod peas and 1 teaspoon butter in a second covered casserole. Cook in the microwave oven, stirring once, until tender (about 5 minutes). Pour the contents of the casserole into the onions.

223

If an undesirable amount of liquid has accumulated, drain the liquid into a small dish or casserole. Reduce the liquid by cooking a minute or two in the microwave oven. The butter will remain in the dish. Stir the butter that remains, the salt, and the pepper into the vegetables. If the vegetables have cooled a little, they may be reheated for 1 minute in the microwave oven.

Tip: the onions are cooked first because they are more dense than the peas and can use the standing time, which they will get while the peas are cooking. It is too difficult to get both vegetables to the desired degree of doneness if they are cooked together.

My Time Is _____ *Min.*

SAUTÉED SNOW PEAS

Whether you buy them under the name of Chinese peas, snow peas, or edible pod peas, these are a delightful vegetable. They not only go with Oriental dishes, but they complement any food.

Makes 4 servings
  2 strips bacon
  2 cups edible pod peas

Preparation time 10 Min.
Salt to taste
Pepper to taste

Put the bacon in a casserole and cook, uncovered, until crisp (about 2 to 3 minutes), in the microwave oven. Set the bacon aside on a piece of paper toweling. Discard all the bacon fat except for 1 tablespoon. Add the pod peas to the bacon fat and cook, covered, stirring from time-to-time, until the pod peas are bright green and just barely tender. Crumble the bacon and add to the peas. Season to taste. If frozen pod peas have been used, add 1 teaspoon cornstarch for thickening when you start cooking the peas.

Tip: a delightful addition is 1/2 cup sliced water chestnuts or 1/4 cup finely-chopped onion cooked in with the peas. Another time, try 1/2 cup chopped mushrooms; or how about 1/4 cup chopped cashew nuts. There is no end to the interesting variations.

224

My Time Is _____ *Min.*

BLACK EYE PEAS AND SOW BELLY

In some parts of our country it is believed that eating Black Eye Peas and Sow Belly on New Year's Day will bring good, luck for the rest of the year. But don't reserve this "Soul Food" recipe for this holiday only. It is good, hearty eating the year around.

Makes 4 servings	*Preparation time 30 Min.*
1/4 pound salt pork (or sow belly) or more as desired	1/4 teaspoon powdered sage
2 cups hot tap water	1 package (10 ounces) black eye peas, frozen or fresh

Dice the salt pork and rinse well. Drain. Put into a large casserole and cook, stirring occasionally, until the pork is done and starts to brown lightly. (This should take about 4 to 5 minutes.) Discard all but 2 to 4 tablespoons of the pork fat. Slowly add the hot water. The hot water is needed to keep the casserole from cracking. Add the sage and black eye peas. Cook, covered, stirring every 5 minutes, until the peas are tender. This should take from 20 to 25 minutes depending on how starchy and mature the peas are. Let stand 5 minutes before serving.

225

Tip: if using fresh, shelled black eye peas, since these rarely come in 10-ounce packages, adjustments will have to be made in the cooking time, as well as in the amounts of the other ingredients, in accordance with the amount being cooked.

My Time Is _____ Min.

POTATOES, WHITE

The potato ranks eighth in importance in the world's food crops. There are many varieties grown, some suitable to the tropics, and some to the temperate zones. Some bear early and some late.

Potatoes were introduced into Europe in the latter part of the 16th century from South America. By the end of the 17th century they were a major crop in Ireland. The name, potato, came to us from the Indian "batata," through the Spanish "patata," into English as potato.

Potatoes are high in vitamins A and C and in iron, calcium, and phosphorous. Actually, potatoes themselves are not high in calories. It is all those other good things cooked with or served with the potato that are so fattening.

Selection

Choose firm, succulent, smooth-skinned potatoes regardless of the variety selected. For baking potatoes choose uniformly shaped potatoes for more even cooking. Avoid soft or wrinkled potatoes, bumpy ones, those that have started to sprout, and those with blemishes.

Preparation

Wash and drain the potatoes. For baked potatoes, it is sometimes necessary to use the services of a scrub brush. If the potato is to be baked, no other preparation is necessary.

For other potato dishes, pare the potatoes, cut out any "eyes" and blemishes, and then rinse. The potatoes may be cooked whole, cut up, sliced, diced, or whatever.

Cooking

Fresh

Baked potatoes are more moist when cooked in the microwave oven. If a drier potato is desired, prick deeply with a long-tined fork to let excess moisture escape as steam. Potatoes baked in their own skin do not need to be covered. That skin is the cover.

When you are baking only 1 or 2 potatoes, that is the time to choose the most uniformly-shaped and perfectly-formed potato possible for even cooking. When 3 or more potatoes are being cooked at one time, then use the irregularly-shaped potatoes. Arrange them like the spokes of a wheel with the heavy part of the potato to the outer edge and the smaller end of the potato toward the hub of the wheel. IMPORTANT: halfway through the cooking period, turn each potato over. Keep the small end of the potato still toward the wheel hub. Potatoes are quite dense and this procedure allows for even cooking of both sides of the potato.

The potatoes are done when they are a little tender but still firm. Allow at least 5 minutes standing time for the residual cooking to take place. The potatoes will soften greatly during this period. Signs of overcooking are gummy potatoes or those having a dry honey-combed appearance.

One medium potato will cook in about 4 to 5 minutes. Two in 7 to 8 minutes, 3 in 10 to 12 minutes, and 4 in 14 to 16 minutes. Ones definition of "medium" will also affect the overall cooking times.

For potatoes that are peeled, put them in a casserole with 1/4 cup water. Stir them twice during the cooking period. About 2 minutes before the potatoes are done, rearrange the pieces. Push the more tender pieces to the center and the less tender pieces to the outer edge. In potatoes, time must always be allowed for residual cooking. If the potatoes become gummy, they have been overcooked. One pound of potatoes cooks in about 10 to 11 minutes. One-and-one-half pounds takes about 15 minutes.

French fries cannot be cooked in the microwave oven.

Frozen

Potatoes do not freeze well so they are not often frozen. Most of those available are small, whole potatoes or prebaked ones.

Put the whole potatoes and 1/4 cup water in a covered casserole. Cook in the microwave oven until almost tender, stirring twice. Shortly before they are done, push the more tender pieces to the center and the less tender pieces to the outer edge. Allow 5 minutes standing time after cooking. Times are similar to unfrozen potatoes.

For prebaked potatoes, wrap in wax paper or plastic wrap. Defrost and then heat thoroughly.

Canned

Canned potatoes are fully cooked and only need heating before using.

Seasonings:	basil, caraway, celery seed, chives, dill, onion, paprika, parsley, rosemary, scallions, butter, salt, pepper
Sauces:	Béchamel, Cheese, Mornay, Parsley, Velouté and White sauces; sour cream
Cheeses:	American, Cheddar, Cream, Gruyère, Monterey Jack, Swiss
Extra serving suggestions:	hot, with caraway and grated Cheddar cheese
	hot, in sour cream with peas
	hot, in cream with grated Monterey Jack cheese and finely-chopped rosemary

229

MASHED POTATOES

If it seems strange to find a recipe for mashed potatoes, it is here for two reasons. One, very few people think of cooking the potatoes for mashing in the microwave oven. Two, because there are two simple but very important points to doing it well. Look at the time saved. Preparation time in conventional cooking is about 55 minutes. In the microwave oven, just 25.

Makes 4 generous servings		*Preparation time 25 Min.*
1 1/2	pounds white potatoes	2 tablespoons butter or
1/4	cup water	margarine
	Salt to taste	3/4 cup hot milk
	White pepper to taste	(approximately)

Pare and wash the potatoes. Cut them into uniform-sized pieces. Put the potatoes and water in a covered casserole. Here is important point number 1. Cook in the microwave oven until medium tender, never soft (about 12-15 minutes). Stir twice during the cooking period. Then, about 2 minutes before the potatoes are done, rearrange them by pushing the tender pieces to the center and the less tender pieces to the outer edge. Now comes important point number 2. Let stand 5 minutes, covered, before mashing. This allows residual cooking to take place. Heat the milk.

230

Add the butter, salt, and pepper. Mash until smooth. Start mashing in the hot milk gradually. When the proper texture has been reached, whip the potatoes well with a large spoon to make them fluffy. If need be, reheat for a minute or two before serving.

Tip: if the potatoes are cooked to the degree of tenderness of conventionally cooked potatoes, the residual cooking will cause overcooked potatoes, in which case the potatoes will be gummy. Allowing the residual cooking before the mashing makes the potatoes tender enough to mash smoothly, ensuring no lumps.

My Time Is _____ Min.

BALKAN POTATO SOUP

This rich, hearty potato soup is very easy to prepare. Try it on a cold winter's eve or any time the weather is nippy and a rich satisfying soup is in order.

Makes 8 servings

- 4 slices bacon, diced
- 1/4 cup chopped mushrooms
- 1/4 cup chopped parsley
- 1 cup chopped onion
- 1 clove garlic, minced
- 2 teaspoons salt
  Pepper to taste

Preparation time 45 Min.

- 1/4 teaspoon thyme leaves
- 4 cups peeled and diced
  white potatoes
- 3/4 cup water
- 4 tablespoons flour
- 4 cups rich milk

Cook the bacon in a 2 1/2- to 3-quart casserole, uncovered, for 4 minutes. With a slotted spoon, dip out the bacon pieces and reserve. Add the mushrooms, parsley, onion, garlic, salt, pepper, and thyme to the bacon drippings. Stir, cover, and cook 4 minutes. Stir in the bacon pieces and the potatoes. Add the 3/4 cup water. Cook, covered, in the microwave oven until barely tender (about 15 minutes), stirring several times.

231

Mix a little of the milk with the flour until a thin paste is formed. Add the flour mixture to the milk. Stir it into the potatoes. Cover, cook in the microwave oven until the soup is thickened and the milk is hot (about 12 to 15 minutes), stirring several times to keep the flour in suspension.

Tip: float a pat of butter on each bowl of soup; sprinkle on a dash or two of paprika for that extra richness and color.

My Time Is _____ *Min.*

POTATOES ESPAÑOL

The mint, peas, and parsley give a nice green tint to this potato dish. Try it as a side dish to lamb.

Makes 4 to 6 servings
Preparation time 25 Min.

- 3 tablespoons olive or salad oil
- 2 cloves garlic, finely minced
- 6 potatoes, peeled and thinly sliced
- 2 teaspoons mint, finely cut
- 1/2 cup fresh or frozen peas
- 1 teaspoon salt
- Pepper to taste
- 1/4 cup finely-chopped parsley
- 1/4 cup water

Put the oil and garlic in a covered casserole and cook in the microwave oven 3 minutes. Add the potatoes, mint, peas, salt, pepper, and half of the parsley. Stir to coat evenly with the oil. Add the water. Cook, covered, in the microwave oven for 10 minutes. Very gently stir to put the outer part of the potatoes into the center and the inner part to the outside. Cover and continue cooking in the microwave oven until the potatoes are almost completely tender (about 5 minutes). Let stand 5 minutes before serving. Garnish with the remaining parsley.

232

Tip: use 1/2 teaspoon dried mint leaves, well crumbled, in place of the fresh, if the fresh is not available.

My Time Is _____ Min.

POTATOES AND ONIONS

In the following recipe you have a choice. Serve the vegetables with or without a sauce. It is good both ways and will allow for variety.

Makes 6 servings
  1 pound potatoes
  1/4 cup water
  1/2 pound tiny boiling onions
  1 tablespoon butter

Preparation time 20 Min.
  Salt and pepper to taste
  1 cup sauce (White, Cheese, Béchamel, or Parsley)
     optional

Peel and rinse the potatoes. Dice into 1-inch cubes. Put the potatoes and water in a covered casserole. Cook in the microwave oven, stirring twice, until tender (about 10 minutes). Set the potatoes aside.

While the potatoes are cooking, peel and rinse the onions. Put the onions and butter in a covered casserole. Cook in the microwave oven, stirring once, until tender (about 5 to 6 minutes).

Add the onions to the potatoes. If they are to be served without a sauce, drain the liquid into a small dish or casserole and reduce by boiling in the microwave oven. Add the remaining liquid and butter back to the vegetables. Add the salt and pepper. Stir gently to mix. If needed, reheat the vegetables for a minute or two in the microwave oven.

If sauce is to be added, drain the liquid from the vegetables and use it as part of the liquid when making the sauce. After the sauce is made, gently stir it into the vegetables. If needed, the vegetables may be reheated for a minute or two in the microwave oven.

Tip: cook the potatoes first, as they need the longer standing time. Be careful not to overcook the potatoes.

233

My Time Is _____ Min.

PARSLIED POTATOES

Follow the recipe directions to not only make a flavorsome dish but also to retain all the nutrients. Red potatoes or new potatoes are especially good this way.

Makes 4 servings	*Preparation time 15 Min.*
1 pound potatoes	1/4 cup minced parsley
1/2 cup water	Salt and pepper to taste
2 tablespoons butter	

Peel, wash, and dice the potatoes. Put into a covered casserole with the water. Cook until tender (about 8 to 12 minutes), stirring several times for even cooking, in the microwave oven. Drain the water from the potatoes into a small casserole or dish. Set the potatoes aside.

Add the butter to the water and cook, uncovered, in the microwave oven until the liquid is thick. Stir the parsley into the butter. Add the parsley-butter mixture, salt, and pepper to the potatoes. Stir to coat the potatoes thoroughly.

234 **Tip:** for a surprising bit of crunch and a flavor change, add either 1/2 teaspoon poppy seed or 1/4 teaspoon celery seed. Yummy.

My Time Is _____ *Min.*

ROAST DRIPPING POTATOES

Cook potatoes in the drippings from a roast or in bacon drippings. They pick up the meat flavor and they are tender. A bit of paprika makes them look almost browned.

Makes 4 servings
1 to 1 1/2 pounds potatoes
1/4 cup or more roast or
    bacon drippings
  2 teaspoons finely-chopped
    green onion

Preparation time 15 Min.
2 slices crisply-cooked
    bacon, finely crumbled
Salt and pepper to taste
Paprika

Pare the potatoes and cut into pieces. Try to have the pieces of a uniform size for even cooking. Put the potatoes and the drippings in a casserole or in the roasting dish. Coat well with the fat of the drippings. Cook 3 minutes. Stir to coat again with the drippings. Cook 3 minutes more. Stir to coat again with the drippings. Cook 3 minutes more. Remove the potato pieces that are done to a serving dish and continue cooking any that need it, until they are done too. Remove them to the serving dish.

Add the green onion, bacon, salt, and pepper. Sprinkle with paprika and toss gently to mix and coat. Add more paprika, if needed.

235

Tip: if you have just cooked a roast, add any vegetables, such as the potatoes, after the roast has been removed and is having its standing time. Coating the vegetables with the drippings improves the flavor and seals their moisture in, eliminating the need for covering.

My Time Is _____ *Min.*

SQUASH, SUMMER

Summer squash are quick-growing, small-fruited types of squash. They are high in water content, so they do not store well. They are very low in calories. The range of shapes, sizes, and colors is remarkable. The most common kinds of summar squash are pan, crook-neck, and zucchini. The colors range from pale green to dark green to yellows.

The fruits develop rapidly and are harvested while quite immature. The entire fruit is eaten, as the skin and seeds are very soft and tender at this stage.

Selection

Summer squash are the tender, immature fruit of certain varieties of squash.

Whether you are selecting zucchini, pan squash, crook-neck, straight-neck, or any other succulent squash, look for young, tender, succulent fruits with good color. Avoid overaged, wilted, or blemished squash.

Preparation

Wash and drain the fruit. No paring is necessary. Cut off any blemishes. Cut off the stem and the blossom ends. The squash may be used whole, sliced, or cut up.

Cooking

Fresh

Put the squash in a covered casserole. Cook in the microwave oven until tender. If whole squash are being cooked, turn them over and rearrange them once during the cooking period, putting the less tender ones to the outer edge and the more tender ones to the center. If the squash are not whole, stir them gently twice during the cooking period. Squash cook very fast and great care should be taken to not overcook them. With the residual cooking, they can become overcooked and mushy very quickly.

One pound of squash, thickly sliced, needs about 7 to 8 minutes cooking. One-and-one-half pounds cooks in 8 to 9 minutes. Thin slicing tends to speed up the cooking.

Frozen

Put the frozen squash, icy-side up, in a covered casserole. Cook in the microwave oven, stirring once, until tender. A 10-ounce package will cook in 7 to 8 minutes.

Canned

Not available canned.

Seasonings:	caraway, dill, garlic, marjoram, onion, parsley, sesame seed, butter, salt, pepper
Sauces:	Allemande, Bearnaise, Butter and Seed, Cheese, Garlic, Hollandaise, Hot Poppy Seed, Mornay, Parsley, Tomato
Cheeses:	American, Cheddar, Cream, Farmer, Gruyère, Monterey Jack, Mozzarella, Parmesan, Provolone, Romano, Swiss
Wines:	chablis, rhine wine, sauterne, sherry
Nuts:	almonds, brazil nuts, filberts, pine nuts, pumpkin seed, sunflower seed
Extra serving suggestions:	hot, with garlic, butter, salt, and pepper
	hot, with butter, Parmesan cheese, salt, and pepper
	hot, with mayonnaise, lemon juice, garlic, and dill
	raw, with cold Garlic sauce

SUMMER SQUASH CASSEROLE

Here is a blend of two types of summer squash in a dish that is almost a meal in itself. You will want to serve this often as long as the squash is available.

Makes 6 servings

1 cup chopped onion
1 clove garlic, minced
1 tablespoon butter or margarine
2 cups bite-sized pieces of zucchini squash
2 cups bite-sized pieces of crook-neck squash
1/3 cup cracker crumbs

Preparation time 25 Min.

1/3 cup grated Parmesan cheese
1/4 teaspoon salt
2 teaspoons crushed basil leaves
Pepper to taste
2 eggs, beaten
2 cups milk

Put the onion, garlic, and butter in a covered casserole. Cook in the microwave oven for 3 minutes. Stir in the two types of squash. Cook, covered, stirring twice, until tender (about 7 minutes). In a small bowl, mix the cracker crumbs, Parmesan cheese, salt, basil, and pepper. In another small dish gradually blend the milk into the beaten egg. Gradually beat the egg-milk mixture into the cracker crumbs. Gently stir the final mixture into the squash. Cook, covered, for 4 minutes in the microwave oven. Stir gently. Cook, covered, for 4 minutes more or until set. Allow 5 minutes standing time.

239

Tip: this will set best if it is put into an 8″ × 8″ baking dish that has a small glass set in the center of it. Pour the ingredients carefully around the glass after the final mixing.

My Time Is _____ *Min.*

ZUCCHINI BRAZILIAN STYLE

A hint of sweetness and a hint of meat sauce give this zucchini recipe from Brazil a unique flavor. Try it, you'll like it.

Makes 4 servings   *Preparation time 20 Min.*

2 slices bacon, diced	1 teaspoon sugar
3 tablespoons minced onion	1/4 teaspoon salt
1/3 cup finely-chopped green pepper	1/8 teaspoon pepper
1/2 teaspoon Kitchen Bouquet (or other meat glaze)	2 large zucchini

In a rectangular dish, long enough to hold the zucchini, cook the bacon until it is crisp (about 2 or 3 minutes). Add the onion, green pepper, Kitchen Bouquet, sugar, salt, and pepper. Cook, covered with wax paper or plastic wrap, for 6 minutes.

Cut off and discard the ends of the zucchini. Cut the zucchini in half, lengthwise. Place in the dish with the sauce and spoon the sauce over them. Cook, covered, in the microwave oven about 5 to 7 minutes or until the desired degree of doneness is obtained. **240** Serve them with the sauce spooned on top.

Tip: do not cook the zucchini quite as tender as you desire it, as residual cooking will finish the cooking during the time it takes to get everyone seated at the table and served. Zucchini cooks so quickly that care must be taken not to overcook it.

My Time Is _____ Min.

ZUCCHINI IN CREAM AND TARRAGON

The French have a way with vegetables. The cream adds a touch of richness, and the tarragon, a different tang. Try this at any time of the year, but especially try it in the summer when an ample supply of tender young zucchini is available.

Makes 4 servings

2 1/2 pounds zucchini
4 tablespoons butter
Salt and pepper to taste
2 tablespoons minced shallots or green onions
1 teaspoon fresh, minced tarragon (or 1/4 teaspoon dried)

Preparation time 15 Min.

1 cup or more heavy cream
2 tablespoons minced parsley
1 teaspoon fresh, minced tarragon (or 1/4 teaspoon dried)

Wash the zucchini and cut into slices or desired shape. Put the zucchini, butter, salt, pepper, shallots, and 1 teaspoon tarragon in a covered casserole and cook in the microwave oven, stirring occasionally to redistribute the heat evenly, until the zucchini is almost tender (about 6 to 8 minutes). Add enough cream to coat the zucchini, but not enough to flood it. (Cream may be thickened slightly with flour, if desired, but it should not be a thick sauce.) Bring it to a simmer. Sprinkle on the remaining tarragon and the parsley.

241

Tip: evaporated milk may be used in place of the heavy cream, if desired. The size and maturity of the zucchini will affect the cooking time. Take care not to overcook, as zucchini should be tender-firm, never mushy, and there will be some residual cooking.

My Time Is _____ Min.

ZUCCHINI PARMESAN

For the best results with this recipe, do not cook the zucchini past the crisp, crunchy stage. The zucchini should have just barely softened and been heated through when it is taken from the oven. The crunch and the flavor combinations are what make zucchini parmesan so delightful.

Makes 4 servings　　　　　　　　　*Preparation time 10 Min.*

1/4　cup chopped onion
　2　tablespoons butter or
　　　margarine
　1　pound zucchini, sliced
　　　very thin

1/4　cup grated Parmesan
　　　cheese
Salt and pepper to taste

Put the onion and butter in a covered casserole. Cook in the microwave oven for 3 minutes. Add the zucchini and stir. Cook, covered, stirring every 2 minutes, until the zucchini has just begun to soften (about 4 1/2 to 5 minutes). Add the Parmesan cheese, salt, and pepper. Stir gently to coat evenly. Serve.

242 **Tip:** if you are a devotee of garlic, put 1 small clove garlic, minced, in with the onion. An alternate method of preparing the zucchini is to dish out the servings and then sprinkle the cheese over the servings.

My Time Is _____ Min.

ZUCCHINI AND TOMATOES

This is a very traditional way to fix zucchini. The beautiful color and flavor contrasts add to the enjoyment of this dish. If your family is big on zucchini, double the recipe and increase the cooking time.

Makes 4 servings

1/4 cup minced onion
1 tablespoon butter
3 medium-sized zucchini, sliced

Preparation time 15 Min.

1 can (1 pound) tomatoes
Salt and pepper to taste

Cook the onion with the butter in a covered casserole in the microwave oven until tender (about 3 to 4 minutes). Add the juice from the tomatoes and reduce by boiling, uncovered, in the microwave oven. Add zucchini and cook until almost tender. Add tomatoes, salt, and pepper, and cook, covered, until heated through.

Tip: try substituting fresh tomatoes for the canned. Use about 3 to 4 medium-sized tomatoes. Peel and chop them and add them in at the same time as the zucchini. Be careful not to overcook the vegetables; allow for the residual cooking that will take place. Vegetables are best when they are at the tender-crisp stage.

243

My Time Is _____ Min.

SQUASH, WINTER

Winter squash are usually large, hard-rinded, and store well for long periods of time. The flesh is usually a shade of orange, indicating it is high in vitamin A. Pumpkins are a form of squash, in fact, in Spanish there is only one word for pumpkins and squashes—*calabasa*.

Hard squash are grown extensively in the New World as they are native to the area. They have an affinity with anything that goes with pumpkin and can even be made into pie (as pumpkins are).

When it is necessary to cut a small squash, one that will be cooked in its entirety, cook it about three-fourths of the way done in the microwave oven before trying to cut it open. It will cut very easily then and there will be no chance of the knife slipping and cutting you.

Selection

Winter squash are the hard, mature fruit of certain varieties of squash. Most varieties are very large, therefore they are cut and sold by the piece. There are exceptions such as the acorn and Danish squash, which are small and sold uncut.

For squash sold by the piece, look for signs that the fruit is freshly cut. The meat should be firm and well colored. Avoid pieces that are too soft, that appear damp and dark colored, or show any signs of being cut too long ago.

For whole squash, except at the end of the season, the choice is more to find the right-sized squash. Look for well-formed, globular squash that will allow for more even cooking. Sometimes late in the season the squash may start to get soft and shriveled. Avoid these if possible.

Preparation

To prepare cut pieces of squash, rinse and blot dry. If the piece is to be cooked as is, it may be peeled or not as you wish. If the piece is to be cut up, it should be peeled and diced into the desired sized cubes, after removing the seeds and the material around the seeds.

For squash to be cooked whole, no preparation other than the washing is needed.

Cooking

Fresh

If a piece of squash is to be cooked whole, put it in a shallow baking dish and cover it with wax paper or plastic wrap. If it is quite thick, start cooking it skin-side up. Halfway through the cooking period, turn it over. If the piece of squash is fairly thin, cook it skin-side down from the beginning. When the squash is beginning to get tender, add whatever seasoning ingredients, butter, brown sugar, spices, etc., that are to be used. Cook until moderately tender to allow for the residual cooking. One-and-one-half pounds of squash will cook in about 9 to 10 minutes. Allow 5 minutes standing time.

If the piece of squash is to be cooked, cut into small pieces, pare and dice it. Put it in a covered casserole. Cook it in the microwave oven, stirring twice, until tender. One-and-one-half pounds of squash cooks in 9 to 10 minutes. Allow 5 minutes standing time. If desired, the squash may be mashed after the standing time is over.

246

If a squash is to be cooked whole, put it in the microwave oven and cook it until it is slightly tender on the under-side (about 3 to 4 minutes after cooking starts). Turn it over, continue cooking until the squash is slightly tender. Take it out of the oven and cut it in half. Scoop out the seeds and the stringy material that surrounds the seeds. Put the squash halves back in the oven. Seasoning ingredients, butter, brown sugar, spices, etc., may be added at this time. Cover with wax paper or plastic wrap. Cook until tender. Two squash weighing about 1 1/2 pounds will need 8 to 10 minutes cooking time.

Frozen

Frozen squash comes precooked. Put it, icy-side up, in a covered casserole. Cook in the microwave oven, stirring twice, until the squash is defrosted and thoroughly heated. A 12-ounce package will thaw and heat in about 7 minutes. Two packages take about 12 minutes and need stirring more often.

Canned

If squash comes canned it is fully cooked and only needs heating before using.

Seasonings:	allspice, cardamom, cinnamon, clove, lemon, nutmeg, pumpkin pie spice, sesame seed, butter, salt, pepper, sugar, brown sugar, honey, molasses
Sauces:	Hot Orange
Wines:	chablis, port, rhine wine, rosé, sauterne, sherry, tokay, vermouth
Nuts:	almonds, brazil nuts, coconut, filberts, peanuts, pecans, pine nuts, pistachios, pumpkin seed, sunflower seed, walnuts
Extra serving suggestions:	hot, with Orange sauce and topped with toasted coconut
	hot, as a pudding made with eggs, milk, sugar, and spices (cardamom, cinnamon, clove, or such)
	hot, mashed with butter and brown sugar and clove
	hot, cooked with apples and cinnamon and sugar

SQUASH WITH PINEAPPLE

Use small servings of this squash recipe as it is rich. The pineapple certainly perks up the flavor. Try this as a side dish to ham or pork roast.

Makes 6 servings	*Preparation time 17 Min.*
1 1/2 pounds hard squash	6 tablespoons brown sugar (packed)
6 tablespoons canned, crushed pineapple	2 tablespoons butter or margarine
3 teaspoons cornstarch	

Peel the squash and cut it into bite-sized pieces. Put it in a covered casserole. Cook it in the microwave oven, stirring twice, until tender (about 7 to 9 minutes). Remove from the oven and let stand.

248 Put the pineapple in a small dish or casserole. Stir in and carefully dissolve the cornstarch. Stir in the brown sugar. Add the butter. Cook in the microwave oven, stirring several times, until the mixture boils and thickens. When the sauce has thickened and come to a boil, continue cooking for 2 to 3 minutes more on defrost or low power. If these powers are not available, let the sauce sit for 2 minutes and then cook 1 minute more on high. Stir carefully into the squash. Enough liquid will have formed from the squash to thin out the syrup. Serve.

Tip: for a change of texture, mash the squash after the syrup has been added and then beat smooth. This recipe is good either way.

My Time Is _____ Min.

SQUASH PUDDING

There is just a hint of sweetness and cinnamon in Squash Pudding, but it raises the taste out of the ordinary. Another plus is the short preparation time. Add about 5 minutes to the preparation time if you are using fresh squash.

Makes 4 servings	Preparation time 10 Min.
1 package (12 ounces) frozen, precooked squash	2 tablespoons flour
	1 1/2 tablespoons sugar
	1/2 cup milk
1/2 teaspoon cinnamon	1 egg, beaten

Put the frozen squash in a covered casserole. Cook in the microwave oven until thoroughly defrosted. Mix the cinnamon, flour, and sugar in a small casserole. Gradually stir in the milk. Cook, covered, stirring several times, until the mixture comes to a boil. Continue cooking on defrost or low power for 2 or 3 minutes more. If these powers are not available, let the sauce sit for 2 minutes and then cook 1 minute more on high. Stir a small amount of the hot mixture into the egg yolk. Gradually stir the egg into the hot sauce. Stir the sauce into the squash. Continue cooking, stirring twice, until the mixture thickens and is very hot. Let stand 5 minutes. **249**

If fresh squash is being used, peel and dice it and cook it in the microwave oven in a covered casserole until it is very tender. Mash it thoroughly and proceed as above.

Tip: the flour and egg thicken the squash and give it better consistency while the sugar and cinnamon improve the flavor. Milk adds to the nutrition.

My Time Is _____ Min.

STUFFED ACORN SQUASH

Two vegetables for the price of one, as it were. An easy-to-fix, delightful way to serve small squash, and they look like a dream.

Makes 4 servings

- 2 acorn or danish squash, about 3/4 pound each
- 1 tablespoon butter or margarine
- 2 medium-sized onions, slivered

Preparation time 20 Min.

- 1 green apple, diced
- 1/4 teaspoon celery seed
- 1/2 teaspoon sugar
- 1 tablespoon butter or margarine

Put the squash in the microwave oven, spaced evenly apart. Cook for 5 minutes. Turn the squash over. With a long-tined fork, prick the squash. Cook until tender, about 3 to 5 minutes more. Take the squash from the oven.

Put the 1 tablespoon butter, onions, apple, celery seed, and sugar in a covered casserole. Cook in the microwave oven, stirring several times, until the onions are tender (about 10 minutes).

250 While the onions are cooking, cut the squash in half lengthwise. With a spoon, scoop out the seeds and discard. When the onions are done, divide them evenly, filling the cavities of the squash halves. Top each piece with 1/4 of the remaining tablespoon butter. Put back into the microwave oven and cook 2 minutes more.

Tip: the squash is pricked to keep it from rupturing from the steam pressure that builds up inside during the cooking process. By waiting until the squash is partially cooked, it is easier to prick. Also note how easy it is to cut the squash in two after it has been cooked.

My Time Is _____ Min.

SWEET POTATOES AND YAMS

Sweet potatoes are edible members of the morning glory family. Columbus ate them when he first came to the New World, yet sweet potatoes are almost unknown in Europe as they cannot tolerate the climate there. Many are grown in the southeastern part of the United States and are also found in the Philippines, the East Indies, and much of Southeastern Asia.

The item we know as the yam is not the same as the yam of the tropics, where it is a major item of the diet. Rather the yam we know is a specific form of the sweet potato developed in Puerto Rico. So it can truly be said that all yams are sweet potatoes, but not all sweet potatoes are yams. Yams are sweeter, more moist, and have a deeper orange color than other varieties of sweet potatoes.

Selection

For sweet potatoes to be used as individual servings, choose small uniformly-shaped ones. For recipes that call for them to be cut up or mashed, use the larger ones, if you wish. Regardless of size, select those with smooth skins. Avoid those that have gotten soft or that have blemishes.

Preparation

If the sweet potatoes are to be cooked in their skins, the only preparation is to wash them and to prick them a time or two. If they are to be used in other ways, after washing them, pare off the skin and cut out any purple spots or blemishes. Then cut them as desired. Sometimes sweet potatoes will discolor when they are exposed to the air. For this reason, it is best to wait until the potatoes are to be used before paring them.

Cooking

Fresh

If cooking whole, prick the sweet potatoes to prevent rupturing. If two potatoes are being cooked at one time, place one in each half of the oven. If three or more are being cooked, place them wagon-spoke fashion with the smaller end at the hub of the wheel. Halfway through the cooking period turn them over. Keep the small end still toward the hub of the wheel. If you were fortunate enough to find uniformly-shaped potatoes, then reverse the position of the potatoes, end for end, as well as turning them over. Continue cooking until tender. Let stand 5 minutes.

It is difficult to give cooking times for sweet potatoes as they vary so in size. Also the terms "small" and "medium" mean different things to different people. Weight seems the best criteria. One-and-one-half pounds will cook in 10 to 12 minutes. Two pounds cook in 12 to 14 minutes.

If the potatoes are cut up, they must be covered during the cooking period. Adding 1/4 cup water helps to speed up the cooking. Cooking times will be a little less than those listed in the preceding paragraph for two reasons. First, part of the total mass has been lost through the paring. Second, there is more surface area for the microwaves to enter.

Frozen

Put the sweet potatoes in a covered casserole. Cook in the microwave oven until thawed enough to separate. Put the larger pieces to the outside edge of the container and the smaller pieces in the middle. Halfway through the cooking process, rearrange the pieces as needed, putting the less tender pieces to the outer edge and the more tender ones to the center. Continue cooking until tender. A 12-ounce package will cook in 10 minutes.

Canned

Canned sweet potatoes are fully cooked and only need heating before using.

Seasonings:	allspice, cardamom, cinnamon, clove, ginger, lemon, nutmeg, pumpkin pie spice, sage, sesame seed, butter, salt, pepper, sugar, brown sugar, honey, molasses
Sauces:	Hot Orange; pineapple; marshmallows
Wines:	chablis, port, rhine wine, rosé, sauterne, sherry, tokay, vermouth
Nuts:	almonds, brazil nuts, coconut, filberts, peanuts, pecans, pine nuts, pistachios, pumpkin seed, sunflower seed, walnuts

hot, with Orange sauce and topped with toasted coconut

hot, as a pudding made with eggs, milk, sugar, and spices (cardamom, cinnamon, clove, or such)

hot, mashed with butter and brown sugar

253

SNOW-CAPPED YAMS

A simple touch takes baked yams out of the ordinary. By increasing the number of yams and the amount of topping, any number of people may be served. As the number of yams is increased, the baking time must also be increased.

Makes 4 servings   *Preparation time 10 Min.*

- 4 yams weighing a total of about 1 1/2 pounds
- 1/4 cup drained, crushed pineapple
- 1/2 cup marshmallow topping

Wash the yams. Prick them deeply, once on each side. Arrange them in a spoke fashion with the smaller ends toward the middle. If the smaller ends are very small, overlap them. Cook 5 minutes. Turn the potatoes over but keep the smaller ends toward the center. Continue cooking until the potatoes are tender (about 4 to 6 minutes longer).

254 Cut one slit longitudinally and another crosswise in each potato. Squeeze the potato open. Put 1 tablespoon crushed pineapple and 2 tablespoons marshmallow topping into each potato. Return to the oven and cook 2 minutes more.

Tip: yams must be pricked to prevent them from bursting due to the steam pressure that builds up inside of them. Yams do not need covering when cooked in their skins, as their skins act as the cover.

My Time Is _____ Min.

YAM-STUFFED BANANAS

Use this when you want a hearty vegetable that is exotically different. Plantains (the cooking banana) will be starchier than regular bananas but may be substituted if you wish.

Makes 6 servings   *Preparation time 20 Min.*

6 large green-tipped bananas	1 can (8 ounces) crushed pineapple, drained
2 1/2 cups cooked yams, mashed	1/2 cup chopped, salted peanuts
1 teaspoon salt	1/3 cup crumbled, cooked bacon (or more)
2 tablespoons brown sugar, packed	

Wash, but do not peel, the bananas. Lay them flat and make a slit from one end to the other along the top side. Cut through the banana but not through the bottom skin or through the ends. Remove the banana but do not destroy or break the shell. Mash the fruit. Mix all the ingredients. Put the filling back in the banana shells and place them in a large, rectangular baking dish. Smaller bananas should be placed in the center of the dish and larger ones at the ends. If all bananas are the same size, halfway through the cooking, rearrange the bananas for even cooking. Cook 10 to 15 minutes in the microwave oven or until the mixture is heated through.

255

Tip: 6 to 8 slices of bacon, cooked on paper toweling in the microwave oven for about 1 minute per slice, will make 1/3 cup crumbled bacon. If using raw yams, pierce the skins and bake in the microwave oven for 6 minutes. Turn them over and continue baking for about 6 minutes more or until tender. Scoop the flesh from the skins and mash. If you wish, top with extra crumbled bacon.

My Time Is _____ Min.

TOMATOES

The beautiful red tomato has an interesting history. It developed in the northwestern part of South America and its use spread to Mexico. The first tomatoes to reach Europe and Italy were called *pomi d'oro*, or apple of gold, indicating they were a yellow-colored form. Yellow pear tomatoes are still popular with Italians today. By the end of the 16th century both red and yellow varieties were known throughout Western Europe.

The tomato was considered poisonous, so there was a long time before it was used as a food. It may have been because some of its relatives are poisonous or it may have been due to the itching many people experience after working with the plant, especially when it is wet.

The tomato is a fruit used as a vegetable. It is very high in vitamins A and C.

Selection

Select medium-firm, brightly colored tomatoes that are free of blemishes, cracks, or green areas. They should be heavy for their size. Avoid over-ripe or under-ripe fruit or any that have become soft.

Preparation

Wash the tomatoes gently. If the tomatoes are to be peeled, dip them briefly into boiling water and then into cold. The skins will slip off easily. Skins do not soften during the cooking and are sometimes objectionable. Skins should be left on if the tomato is to be cooked, cut in half, with a topping on it, or if it is to be stuffed. In these cases, the skin gives stability to the tomato. Tomatoes may be cooked whole, halved, sliced, or chopped.

Cooking

Fresh

If you wish the tomato to keep its shape or identity, cook, covered, in the microwave oven only until thoroughly heated through. Tomatoes cook down and lose their identity rapidly with overcooking. It is especially important in these cases to consider the residual cooking effect. If the tomato is to cook down and become a part of a sauce, it will do so easily.

Frozen

Tomatoes are not available frozen.

Canned

Canned tomatoes are fully cooked and only need heating before using.

Seasonings:	allspice, basil, bay, cayenne, celery seed, chili powder, chives, cloves, cumin (comino), garlic, lemon, marjoram, mint, mustard, nutmeg, onion, oregano, paprika, parsley, poppy seed, rosemary, sage, savory, sesame seed, tarragon, thyme, butter, salt, pepper, sugar
Cheeses:	American, Bel Paise, Blue, Cheddar, Cottage, Cream, Farmer, Gouda, Gruyère, Monterey Jack, Mozzarella, Parmesan, Provolone, Ricotta, Romano, Stilton, Swiss
Wines:	chablis, rhine wine, rosé, sauterne, sherry, vermouth
Nuts:	pine nuts, pumpkin seed, sunflower seed, water chestnuts
Extra serving suggestions:	hot, "on the half shell" with Parmesan and chives
	hot, with chopped mint, currents, onions, and pine nuts
	hot, with rosemary and shredded Monterey Jack cheese

BROILED TOMATOES PARMESAN

What a lovely way to prepare tomatoes. The color is exquisite and the flavor is superb.

Makes 4 servings   *Preparation time 10 Min.*

4 tomatoes	1/2 cup dried bread crumbs
2 tablespoons finely-minced onion	3 tablespoons Parmesan cheese
1/8 teaspoon ground marjoram	Salt and pepper to taste
1/4 cup butter or margarine	3 tablespoons minced parsley

Cut the tomatoes in half crosswise and put on paper toweling to drain. In a small bowl combine the onion, marjoram, and butter. Cook, covered, 2 minutes in the microwave oven. Stir in the bread crumbs and cook, uncovered, stirring frequently, until the bread crumbs are browned (about 3 minutes). Stir in the Parmesan cheese. Place the tomatoes, cut-side up, in a 2-quart (12" × 9") dish or casserole. Sprinkle the crumb mixture evenly over the tomatoes. Salt and pepper. Sprinkle on the parsley. Cook, uncovered, in the microwave oven for 3 to 4 minutes or until very hot.

259

Tip: overcooking will make the tomato mushy. Avoid this. The skin is left on to keep the tomato from collapsing as it cooks. Frequent stirring is needed during the browning of the bread crumbs to prevent some of the crumbs from burning.

My Time Is _____ Min.

TOMATOES AND PEPPERS MOROCCAN STYLE

Serve these chilled as a vegetable or as a salad. The hot pepper you use can vary from the hot, New Mexico chili to the milder, California chili. The size of the pinch can also be varied according to your taste.

Makes 4 servings
- 3 green peppers
- 3 cloves garlic, minced
- 3 tablespoons olive oil
- 6 medium-sized tomatoes

Preparation time 25 Min.
- 1/2 teaspoon salt
- 1/2 teaspoon paprika
- Pinch of hot pepper

Put the green peppers under the broiler (or over an open flame) and broil, turning often, until they become soft, cracked, and wrinkled. Plunge them into cold water. Peel off the skins. Open and drain the peppers. Remove the core and seeds. Pour the oil in the bottom of a covered casserole and add the garlic. Cook in the microwave oven 1 minute. Slice the peppers and add to the garlic and oil. Cook, covered, 5 minutes.

260

Plunge the tomatoes into boiling water for 30 to 60 seconds. Plunge into cold water and then remove the skins. Slice and add to the peppers along with the remaining ingredients. Stir gently. Cook, covered, about 6 minutes more or until the tomatoes and peppers are tender. Serve chilled.

Tip: to prepare the boiling water to help peel the tomatoes, heat 1 cup water in a 2-cup measure. Dip the tomatoes in, one at a time. If the water cools down too much, reheat for a few minutes between tomatoes.

RICE-STUFFED TOMATOES

Serve your family both a succulent vegetable and a starchy one, all in one tasty dish. It is pretty and flavorful and comes to you from sunny Italy.

Makes 4 servings   *Preparation time 15 Min.*
- 4 medium-sized tomatoes
- 1/4 teaspoon salt
- 1/2 cup cooked rice
- 2 tablespoons chopped mushrooms
- 1 tablespoon minced onion
- 1 teaspoon capers (optional, but nice)
- 1 tablespoon snipped parsley
- 1/4 teaspoon oregano leaves, crumbled
- Dash of pepper
- 1 teaspoon snipped parsley
- 1 tablespoon olive oil

Remove the stem end and the core of the tomato. Slice off the top of the tomato and reserve. Scoop out the pulp and sprinkle the inside of each tomato with salt. (This will pull the excess moisture out of the tomato shell.) Turn upside-down on paper toweling to drain.

Combine and gently stir all the ingredients except the teaspoon of parsley and the olive oil. Use a covered casserole large enough for the tomatoes to fit in without touching each other. Brush each tomato with oil and put into the casserole. Spoon the filling into each tomato. Brush each tomato top with oil and put on top of the filling. Sprinkle the remaining parsley over the tops of the tomatoes. Cover and cook in the microwave oven about 5 minutes or until heated thoroughly.

261

Tip: use leftover rice or cook 1/4 cup raw rice, 1 teaspoon butter, and 1/2 cup plus 2 tablespoons water in a covered casserole in the microwave oven for 12 minutes. If using leftover rice that has been refrigerated, it is best to cook the stuffed tomatoes 3 minutes, let stand 2 minutes, then cook 2 minutes more. This allows the heat enough time to reach the center of the rice mixture without overcooking the tomato shells.

My Time Is _____ Min.

STUFFED TOMATOES

Want a delightfully different way to prepare tomatoes that are really good? That are pretty? And that will complement your dinner? Try these; you'll be pleased you did.

Makes 6 servings

- 6 tomatoes, medium to medium-large
- 1 cup cracker crumbs
- 2 eggs, beaten
- 1/2 cup melted butter
- 1 tablespoon minced parsley

Preparation time 20 Min.

- 1 tablespoon minced onion
- 1 tablespoon paprika
  Salt and pepper to taste
- 1/2 cup hot water
  Butter

Cut a slice off the top of each tomato and discard. Scoop out the centers. It is easiest if a sharp knife is first used to loosen the sides and then a large spoon is used to scoop out the heart and seeds and the excess juice. Chop the centers. Mix with the cracker crumbs, eggs, butter, parsley, onion, paprika, salt, pepper, and water. Stir well.

262 Put each tomato in a custard cup and fill by dividing the stuffing between the tomatoes. It may be necessary to mound up the filling a bit. Top with a small dab of butter. Put the cups in a circle in the microwave oven. Halfway through the cooking time give each cup a half turn to provide even cooking. Cook until the tomatoes are done and the stuffing is puffy (about 10 minutes).

Tip: if you overcook, the tomatoes will be too soft and the stuffing on top will be tough. The flavor of these tomatoes is scrumptious.

My Time Is _____ Min.

TURNIPS AND RUTABAGAS

The turnip gives us two types of food; the round, fleshy ball of root and the young, growing leaves which are used as a green. Turnips are relatives of the cabbage family. There are two varieties used, the ordinary turnip and the rutabaga, which is also known as the Swedish turnip. The rutabaga actually gives better nutrition than the white turnip, being especially high in vitamins A and C.

Like other members of the cabbage family, turnips are biennials. They are harvested at the end of the first growing season. During the second growing season they flower and set seed.

Selection

Look for well-shaped turnips and rutabagas that are free of blemishes, splits, and cuts. They should be firm and succulent. Avoid those that are soft, have wilted, yellowed leaves, or that are quite large. Large ones are apt to be tough and woody.

Preparation

Wash the turnips or rutabagas. If they have their leafy tops on, cut them off at the root top. Peel them. Turnips and rutabagas may be cooked whole, cut up, or sliced.

Cooking

As turnips and rutabagas usually are available fresh only, no other cooking instructions are given.

Put the turnips or rutabagas and 1/4 cup water in a covered casserole. Cook in the microwave oven, stirring twice, until tender. One-and-one-half pounds will take about 12 minutes to cook. Two pounds cook in about 15 minutes. Maturity, hence density, will appreciably affect cooking time.

Seasonings:	caraway, rosemary, butter, salt, pepper
Sauces:	Allemande, Cheese, Hollandaise, Hot Poppy Seed, Mornay, Parsley, Tomato
Cheeses:	American, Cheddar
Extra serving suggestions:	raw, with dip of mayonnaise, garlic, dill, and lemon juice hot, mashed with butter, salt, and pepper

264

HONEYED RUTABAGAS

Rutabagas, commonly called Swedish turnips, have a nice affinity to the taste of honey. The recipe is simple and easy to do. Rutabagas are a bargain both in price and nutrition.

Makes 4 servings
- 4 medium-small rutabagas (1 to 1 1/2 pounds)
- 1/2 cup water
- 3 tablespoons honey

Preparation time 20 Min.
- 1 tablespoon butter or margarine
- Salt and pepper to taste

Pare and dice the rutabagas into bite-sized pieces. Put all the ingredients into a covered casserole and cook in the microwave oven until just tender. (This should take about 12 minutes depending on the amount and the density.) Stir several times during the cooking cycle to ensure even cooking.

Drain all of the liquid off the rutabagas into a small, open casserole or dish. Return the liquid to the microwave oven and continue cooking until the liquid is reduced to less than 1/4 cup. Pour over the rutabagas and stir to coat well. Serve.

265

Tip: age makes a difference in the density of the rutabaga. The size of the rutabagas affects the amount. Remember, density and amount are the two things that affect cooking time more than anything else.

SHERRIED TURNIP (OR RUTABAGA) CASSEROLE

A taste treat whether made with turnips or rutabagas, try this easy casserole. It even tolerates reheating.

Makes 6 servings

- 2 pounds turnips
- 1/4 cup water
- 1/4 cup chopped parsley
- 2 slices dry bread
- 2 tablespoons butter, melted

Preparation time 20 Min.

- 2 teaspoons sugar
- 1/2 teaspoon salt
- 2 tablespoons sherry wine
- 2 eggs

Peel and thinly slice the turnips. Put the turnips, water, and parsley in a covered casserole. Cook in the microwave oven, stirring several times, until tender. (This should take about 12 to 15 minutes.)

While the turnips are cooking, break the bread into small pieces. Mix together the butter, sugar, salt, bread pieces, wine, and eggs. When the turnips are done, do not drain. Mash them thoroughly. Add the remaining ingredients and stir well to blend evenly. Cook, covered, in the microwave oven for 2 minutes. Stir so as to bring the cooked portion to the center and the center portion to the outside of the casserole. Cover and cook until set, which should take about 3 to 4 minutes more.

Tip: slicing the turnips helps them to cook more evenly and to mash more easily. Very old or mature turnips may take a bit longer to cook. Stirring is necessary for even cooking.

266

My Time Is _____ Min.

INDEX

268